Triune

C.C. Hannett

Spuyten Duyvil
New York City

Announcing my gratitude:

Julianna Buckmiller
Ilsa Olsen
Bryan Edenfield
Derek Glassey
James Nolan
Lydia Swartz
Meredith Myre
Scherezade Siobhan
Dax Edword
Brodric Somers
Aurelia Lavallee
Tod Thilleman

Poems in this collection have appeared in *Dum Dum Zine*, *Drunk Monkeys*, and *Juked*.

© 2018 C.C. Hannett
ISBN 978-1-947980-55-6
Cover art & design by Dax Edword
Author portrait by Brodric Somers

Library of Congress Cataloging-In-Publication Data applied for.

"Fractal dirge drenched in dizzying anemoia. Simulation of slowly waking from a binger to imagined fragments of fleeting victories and failures: images flitting through mind as consciousness scrambles in an absurd attempt to make story, to make harsh lucid sense out of nothingness. It's absolutely beautiful."
    James Nolan

"In *Triune*, there is an earnest integrity that walks hand in hand with something tenebrous, infernal & semiopaque. It is a city of tombs & riddles where every exploration is meant to juggle emotional and psychological valences rather deftly but without being too loud about its own mastery. This book is generous with a staggering and abiding richness of imagination juxtaposed against a stark, Black Mirror-esque conjuration of the contemporary hyperrealities. On some plane, it is a celebration of doubt in all its amorphous profusion. There is unapologetic humor in what can best be described as the Common Weird—like glossing over photos of birds in google's image search. Each poem moves like a poised octopus. Make what you will of that but to me it means that this book has anchored itself in two of poetry's perennial harbors—Illusion & Presence—simultaneously and with undeniable ingenuity."
    Scherezade Siobhan

"How can poetry be a page-turner? Yet this is, without losing any harsh seduction or strange familiarity. You don't know what is going to happen next, but you know how you feel about it."
    Lydia Swartz

"What a weird and moving phantasmagoria of sci-fi surrealism, a poetic memoir in which the author splits open his psyche and creates a beautifully realized cosmos. Hannett's deconstruction of self is scary, messy, dangerous, and done with wit and humility. Above all, this is a work of unbridled imagination, which is rare and vital these days. It's also a crazy fun read."
    Bryan Edenfield

for Mat_

PATHOLOGICAL DISLOCATIONS

MANIFEST DYNASTES

THE IMPOSTERS

PATHOLOGICAL DISLOCATIONS

Words bend our thinking to infinite paths of self-delusion, and the fact that we spend most of our mental lives in brain mansions built of words means that we lack the objectivity necessary to see the terrible distortion of reality which language brings.

Dan Simmons, Hyperion

Pt. I | Oxidized Fortunes

Kiss the earth
And vermin fill your hands and mouth
Yvon Goll

I was a pale little worm
grunting across the carpet.
My body was weak, pinned atop itself.
It ached and tickled at once.
All I could manage were tired undulations,
causing me to grunt some more—
the pleading boar of Wenzhou.
My blood felt muddy;
confused,
it did not know which limb to migrate to.
I attempted to shout for help but I could only
mutter sound puzzles.
It was the afternoon still.
Outside, the cicadas had risen
and were chirping their mechanical
nightingale songs,
flying like miniature aircrafts
operated by drunken pilots,
crashing into my bedroom window.
Maybe they were trying to break the glass and
rescue me.
I could only see out of my left-eye
and what I could see was beige
magnified by ten.
My view was floor level: carpet,
wall, closet.
Thoughts of a stroke filled me
with panic and, not having the means
to turn on my side or lie on my back
to observe beyond peripheries
I was unable to confirm if I was alone in the
room or not.

Had this been done to me?
Thoughts of an attack—
a paralyzing blow to the head.
But who?
I could only be certain that I was in a grim
contortion, drooling and voiceless.
Destined for an eternity of imbroglio,
of pathological dislocations.
If the sun could touch it, it would shake,
and shake it did.
Thoughts of remorse;
I shouldn't have come here.
To this day it is unclear to me
whether I woke or fell gently
back to sleep.

* * *

In my most obscure and unfocused moments
I deliver my troubles to a static fiction.
A yellow candy rabbit
peeps out of my coat pocket
it sneaks me Post-It Notes
w/ little fortunes written on them;
obscure and unfocused fortunes
that I misinterpret.
I stick them everywhere,
read silly aphorisms off the
Post-It Notes I tear
from the Post-It Note coffee table
and Post-It Note dresser—
I am a Post-It Note boy
in a Post-It Note world.
Sometimes they do come to fruition
& when they do
they oxidize a shade
of Scheele's green right before
my varied eyes.

   *   *   *

The white male protagonist
refuses to die;
neither will mine.
LITERALLY.
Because it's satire.
You can get away with anything
when it's categorized as satire.
Michael Quartz is an immortal
addicted to suicide.
He fell in love w/ the concept as
a very young child.
Wait, you mean there's an option?
He didn't know that applied to everyone
but him.
He's a junkie for the noose.
The bridge.
The double-decker bus.
He keeps a portable guillotine
on him at all times.
He dies in such a way
he is permitted to die again.
And I get so lost in him
certain behaviors emanate.
I can't tell if I'm writing my own feelings
or if I'm being influenced by my own writing.
Some people go home and pack a bowl,
others crack open a beer;
I kill myself.

   *   *   *

Too much of myself is in this character,
that's the problem.
Michael Quartz works at a pawnshop.
I worked at a pawnshop for seven years.

Michael Quartz's roommate, Bookman,
is a thieving, enabling POS
whose receding hairline is concealed
beneath a kanekalon wig + a black,
Compton flat bill hat.
He's very insecure of his baldness
and cries—a lot.
I once lived with a similar person.
The Darker Ages.
I take notice of this and work to
shift the narrative,
but I'm so self-absorbed
I can only write about myself.
Nevertheless, I persist.

*   *   *

The admin exemplifies
complete disregard
for the season.
I can only imagine
what it must be like
having to fight for so long
without any resolve
only to be handed someone
else's idea of a consolation.
What it must be like
to navigate this planet
operating heavy machinery
w/ hard-hitting fists.
We came after the fall of the Empire
only to witness the rise of the First Order.
Nothing has changed and more
people should be angry
that our generation is just
a lazy, unoriginal sequel.

*　　*　　*

It is with my imagination
Detective Pluto comes home
to an apartment soaked
in neon and midnight aura.
He has surgically removed his spiritual gates—
they have been wrapped in tinfoil
and placed in the freezer box.
In other words: he has no face.
Detective Pluto sees what he cannot
possibly see.
Detective Pluto hears what he cannot
possibly hear.
His dome is a sweating dollop of putty;
a wet, clay flowerpot set to dry at an angle.
The people of this country
see me as nothing
more than a disposable lump in theory,
and a horrific beast about anywhere else,
he says, speaking out of nothing.
In protest, this is your ugliness;
not mine.
5lbs of crushed ice and a dram
of Laphroaig fill the kitchen sink.
Detective Pluto slumps over the sink bowl.
He dunks what used to be his face,
swirling lustily as he absorbs the peaty,
smoky flavors of the scotch
through his skin.
He drinks sepia through scar tissue.
Have I taken a series of questionable liberties?
I'm not sure.
I can't tell if I'm using Detective Pluto
as a catalyst to discuss racism in America
(when it's really not my place)
or if I'm using him
to address elements of my own mental illness.

Maybe both.
I've taken a series of questionable liberties
and I'm prepared to apologize.

*   *   *

When Michael Quartz succumbs
to blood loss or blunt force
trauma
his consciousness temporarily sinks
into the neurodimensional Dead Space.
He is surrounded by Vantablack:
Total darkness.
Nothing above, below; either side of him.
Michael Quartz floats
in the open lufts of redacted sound,
wading in anticipation of
Lady Deathfingers' white veil.
He's in love with the Grim Siren
of the Dead Space.
She swims towards him.
She draws him in with her fingers.
She enfolds him until
color interrupts the space with movement
& he is returned to the Living End.
Returned to the pangs of regeneration
& pensive strolls in the wetlands of
gentrification in progress.
The pain is explosive;
it explodes.

*   *   *

Cordell the aye-aye is a woodsy sprite
and much like the yellow candy rabbit,
has unfathomable powers of clairvoyance,
only it has no clue on how to use these powers.
For centuries the lemur has been unintentionally

murdering humans in its quest to connect w/ us
via fate decryption.
It corners its victims in the shower, when they are
most vulnerable. It paralyzes them with the tapered light
from the flame of its magical Tsetse candle.
You are glued stiff under the shower head;
the hot water has run warm to cold.
The furry gremlin climbs up your limbs,
your torso is upwrenched and crosshatched
in its ghastly taking of you.
It flicks and taps at your glabella
then gnaws a small hole, wide enough to bore
its special narrow middle-finger.
Foraging begins.
It snakes your brains out.
Gummy morsels of brain stick to the tip
of the aye-aye's witchy terminus.
It licks for a taste of your future.
But there's no future to taste.
You're fucking dead.
The fortune never comes to the aye-aye
and it doesn't know why.
I don't understand what I'm doing wrong.

*   *   *

Mountain ranges reveal their curves
as Quartz and the candy rabbit continue on
their deep, locomotive cut
into the tracks.
Michael attempts to discern
acute details among the plentiful gradations
of white snow, pewter, and tree brush stampeding
past and within the smear
of a clear, crisp view he wiped on the window
with his sleeve
as fluffs of condensation
begin to accumulate.

The shape of its frame appears to him
that of a soft spaceship.
An old man eating his own beard.
Quartz imagines an invisible person
running alongside the train
at breakneck velocity; panting,
leaping over bushes and swinging
from power lines.
What if,
like his father
and his father before him,
Quartz embraced his condition?
What would that look like,
he thinks to himself.
No one remembers the stunt man.

*   *   *

A good antagonist is a funhouse mirror
& reflection of the hero.
Isn't it always the tragedies that keep us
going?
Cordell is as exceptional as the yellow candy rabbit
but incapable of progressing beyond
its lethal methods of percussive foraging
as it is an instinctual response.
This is what the aye-aye does.
This is what the aye-aye has always done.
Cordell and Michael Quartz
are opposite ends of the same coin.
Michael Quartz is in search of a higher purpose.
With great power comes great responsibility.
Everyone Cordell tries to help ends up dying.
Michael Quartz can't die.
Michael Quartz wants a path laid out for him.
The yellow candy rabbit can already do this.
But if he gives himself up to Cordell,
he saves countless lives.
Obscure and unfocused lives.

                    *   *   *

So what happens then?
Cordell kills the yellow candy rabbit.
Cordell squeezes it so hard, streams of sugary goo
squirt out the top and bottom of its zombie-like
hand.
Cordell tosses the yellow candy rabbit into a microwave
plugged into a generator
inside of a tent they pitched on a lowly dock in Bridgeport.
They hit start.
Nuclear s'mores, Cordell snickers.
Michael Quartz surrenders himself to the aye-aye.
He surrenders himself to Cordell's plunging, spidery middle-finger.
He surrenders himself to intervals of nerve-wracking pain;
dull twinges of maze-running pain
that will last the lifespan of the aye-aye,
which is unknown.
The pain is explosive;
it explodes.

                    *   *   *

I've always struggled with foundation.
My mother had me when she was 42, which, at that age, increases
your risks to a whole slew of complications and defects—including
exhaustion and a staggering loss of appetite for adventure.
And I can only imagine the harsh cold reality of the impending
struggle that set in when she and my father divorced the following
year.
I was born to six half-siblings, which would later become nine.
My eldest brothers and sisters had already grown up and were mar-
ried and had children of their own by the time of my arrival.
One would assume a person who grew up with that many siblings
and nieces and nephews wouldn't have trouble acclimating to new
environments, that I'd be a boisterous extrovert.
This was not the case for me.
My relationship with my family is much akin to the high turnover

rate experienced in the restaurant industry.

Everyone had dispersed, even my father.

He left to make a third—and final—attempt at starting a family that *fit,* and made no memorable efforts to stay in touch.

I didn't see him again until I was twelve and I haven't seen him since.

At the age of three, my mother and I moved from Lancaster, CA

>> Catalina Island

>> Spokane, WA

>> Tacoma, WA

>> Graham, WA

>> Eatonville, WA

We finally anchored ourselves to [South] Everett, WA when I was seven.

But even then my mother was so restless and impulsive, we were always moving from one apartment complex to the next.

From Casino Rd to Holly Dr.

From Deer Creek to Mallard Cove.

From the F building to the C building.

From the first floor to the very top and back down again.

One transition after the next.

My mother began to notice the difficulties I had making friends so she did her best to provide me a revolving door of emotional support animals.

I had a guinea pig that died of heart failure.

I had a pair of gerbils that escaped from their wire cage daily.

My mother was so terribly frustrated having to hunt for them in the kitchen cupboards and underneath the furniture, she forced me to give them away to our neighbor who, a month later, told me one of the gerbils bit his dad and, in an act of heated retaliation, cut both their tails off with a butcher knife and threw them in the dumpster.

I had a rabbit that pooped turd pellets on the carpet every time it hopped.

My mom couldn't live with that either.

I don't know what happened to the rabbit.

Maybe it turned to candy.

I had a hamster whose urine had an "irregular smell" so it had to go, too.

At this point I had finally made a steady friend whose family agreed to take in the hamster.

Not even a week later my friend called me in a fit of tears apologizing because his dog ripped it apart like a ragdoll.

I had a rat that died suddenly of respiratory complications my first day of Sophomore year. I was convinced it was a bad omen and never went back.

I won't tell you the story about the pig the same way I wasn't told the story about the pig until I had already finished my bacon.

In my experience the animal is a symbol representing something that has happened or something that is missing.

Pt. II | Nocturnal Pursuit

At best life is walking about in the blood we own.
Kim Kyung Ju

Google image search
returned more results of odd
looking birds than I
could have ever bargained for.

Cousin to the Night-
jar & Frogmouth, the Great Potoo
is a glitch of life in barken
chrysalis; its secret will soon sally
from its perch
like a remote control drone
sheathed in heart attack iris
& sketches of burgundy.
The stump moves and I'm freaking out
— *the hand forgot it was there.*

A person becomes accustomed to boring fowl
who've become entitled to nibbles of *Dave's Killer Bread.*
To revealing the recipe that made your dog so cute
people want to:
squeeze it until it poops.

I don't want to say it:
        he's a yorkipoo.

So when an entire gallery of mystical beasts,
purple toads and mountain boomers,
are made into Real Life and available to me,
now that I'm out of fresh episodes of nostalgia,
you have to know I'm going to lose it.

But even then, after awhile,
I grow accustomed. Bored to the detail.

The texture of its pelage is too pronounced
& the lighting—
this isn't a fair representation of the creature's
raw design.

*   *   *

20 yrs later we find Michael Quartz
lining up shot glasses of fluoroantimonic acid
preparing to scare/amuse a house full of party kids.
In order to demonstrate the effects of the corrosive substance,
Michael uses an iPhone to pull up a video of an iPhone
sprinkled with the super acid and plays it
while he sprinkles its screen with his supply of the super acid—
a meta showcase of sizzles and crackles.
Once the demonstration is over,
Michael Quartz slings back shot after shot.
Everyone except for his roommates, the Six brothers,
and his gf, Stacy Mum, watch in terror as Michael kicks
the surrounding cabinets and drawers,
he stomps and claps his hands together
like a train rat busking in Capitol Hill.
Foaming at the mouth, he spits spotty shards
of red hot blood in the faces of the baby-cheeked
party go-ers, freckling the awestruck.
A gothy lumberjack tries to dial 911
But Michael's roommate, Leslie, smacks
the phone from his grasp.
This is all part of the trick, he says.
Just watch. Everything is going to be okay.
Everything is going to be okay.
The gothy lumberjack shakes his head in disbelief.
Party kids are fleeing in mobs of wtf.
Why are you doing this, the gothy lumberjack asks.
He needs to go to a hospital now!
Michael Quartz grabs at the gothy lumberjack,
tugging at the sleeve of his cool black denim.

Wherever you go, there you are,
Michael hisses in the gothy lumberjack's ear.
The gothy lumberjack recoils,
exposing a little double chin.
Abracadabra! Michael croaks.
And then it happens.
He keels over.
He dies in a way so he can die again.

*   *   *

This scene reminds me
of the bizarro tincture—
of Neverland,
the place we go to when we're
young bodied in fingerless
gloves & eyeliner.
We change our names
to Kr33py
to XOXO
Double-fist bottles of 151
& blow
precise streams of fire
& light
novelty-sized cigars.
We transform into donkeys.
Hipster gargoyles on stoops.
Receive pleasure
from questionable sources
we won't remember—
a girl by the name of Star,
the pit is filled with girls
named Star.
We comb the dancing
looking for a girl named Star.
The floor descends into
the Dammit Hole.
All exits have become constellations.

We dream of 7-Eleven
& Taco Bell.
We ration our single packet
of Oriental flavored Top Ramen.
This is nourishment.
It is not much different than
dinner back home.
If you're gonna spew,
spew in this.
The plastic bag has a tear in it
and now there's vomit everywhere.
Flip the mattress over,
spray some Febreeze,
no one will know the difference.
But now there's a circumference
of urine where Star had slept
last night
and you laugh about it w/ friends
who will be memories
of unrequited efforts to cxt
who will be blocked on FB
for reasons long since passed
& forgotten.
I remember crying,
I found a knife under my pillow,
What happened?
Shrug
& you live like this for a while,
if ten yrs is a while.

*   *   *

Madness is not a new invention. . .
I've always been a shy,
introverted, lonely
& sensitive child
who has been perplexed
by human connectivity.

How to sustain lasting,
meaningful friendships.
I never know if it's
because I'm too difficult to read,
or I'm reading too much into
everything
that repels a consistency
I can rely on.
One impractical and unintentional move
is surely at fault:
My trying to fill in the outlines
of a family I knew existed
but never had.
All the mysterious brothers
& sisters
& father
I didn't know; I worked
to replace them
with friends,
establish a bond I'd witnessed
in movies and through my imagination,
what I thought my life would resemble
w/o the rift and complications of
independent beings.
My expectations are too high.
Typical abandonment issues.
I've been a troubled reactionary;
destructive, reckless
conspirator & problematic
paper tiger.
How far has that taken me,
and how far have I grown from
those rampaging steads,
sinking my teeth into
the camel's back.
I've put away my glitter mask.
A literal mask,
spray painted silver

I used to wear
w/ a baby blue XS hoodie
to encapsulate the alien breeze
of surface tension.
What a waste,
blubbering on stairwells
when you're supposed
to be having fun.
I guess I'm on this perpetual loop
of internally unpacking my transgressions,
the bumps in the night,
trying to cope with the reality
of who I am,
who I was,
and their being one in the same.
There are a few, specific incidents
in which I will never exp. closure.

*   *   *

Michael Quartz escaped the poking and prodding
of the aye-aye's
unconventional methods of fortune telling
by simply outliving the deranged little creature.
That is all that is said.
The narrator does not delve into the specifics
of Michael's two decade long
lobotomy or the struggles required
to reconstruct reality as he once knew it.
The headaches, the seizures,
the gumming after words.
How his brain felt like Andouille sausage.
What we focus on now is that he has fully
healed.
Yes, he's traumatized and easily triggered
by the slightest mention or presence
of a Post-It Note,
but he's free to continue on living the life of an

immortal addicted to suicide—on his own terms.
Dying again and again the same way,
waking up revived to the sight
of an evil lemur
mesmerized by a slimy nugget of his brain
displaying holographic visions
of the same future every day:
I see you... Paralyzed by a magical
Tsetse candle...
The whole experience plateaus
after the umpteenth try.
In retrospect, the narrator has contradicted
himself.

*   *   *

Michael has rented a small space
of carpet beneath a poker table
in a party house, which he shares
with his new gf, Stacy Mum.
He doesn't pay rent.
He entertains w/ gratuitous bloodshed.
His performances grant him an endless
supply of boozy juice,
a place to sleep,
and a group of friends as narcissistic
and aloof as the entire
Quartz lineage.
He has resigned himself
and all integrity
to the surf of constant inebriation
& party aesthetics.
Eventually, this too, will plateau.

*   *   *

Enough w/ redundancy.
I want Michael Quartz's

relationship with Stacy Mum
to deviate from typical
cis male romanticism.
Parts of my history
have been rather explorative sexually,
so what if I build on that.
What if, in another time,
let's say when he was nineteen,
Michael Quartz had attempted
to convince an older guy
named Ghee,
whom he'd met through social media,
to let Quartz watch him and his gf
have sex.
Michael was in a voyeuristic phase
and interested in finding a
couple who would consent
to this.
There was something about
two silhouettes converging like
curtains in shadowplay
while the cherry of his cigarette
burned like the fervent,
multi-faceted eye
of the Shrike
in the dark corner of a room.
Ghee thought this idea was really hot
but since he didn't know Quartz,
he had to meet him first and
set probationary rules.
Ghee was very fit.
He was ripped
& cut w/ an Adonis belt.
His gf was a curvaceous platinum blonde—
a french fry dipped in a vanilla milk shake.
They each had one of those digital
'UnHingd' tattoos w/ the special ink
that moves about your body

like a marquee
and erupts in pixels, shuffling
through a series of pre-selected images.
One minute it'd be an epic sleeve
of a kraken eating chow mein,
the next it'd puzzle out into
a chest piece of hieroglyphics.
A 24pk of Rolling Rock in,
Ghee and Quartz were under the sheets
2gether,
Ghee was pulling at his erection
while an infomercial for a rotisserie
played on the TV.
Set it and—
Forget it!
Quartz was just lying there, frozen,
uncertain how to proceed.
The proposition ended the
very moment Ghee ejaculated
without any assistance from Quartz.
Set it and—
Forget it!
Although a bit discouraged by this interaction,
Quartz's fear of touching other erections
soon dissolved.
Upon rumination, Quartz often wonders
if on top of being polyamorous,
he's pansexual.
In that instance,
can I write Stacy as trans?
Should I write her as trans?
Some form of ignorance
must be responsible for spawning
the connection.
I have no desire to fetishize an entire
community.
Stacy is to be loved.
Stacy is to be respected.

Stacy is not a novelty or
a fucking collectible hologram
playing card—
she's a fucking person.
It's all about *intent*.
Intent is key.
Again, I feel I may be taking questionable
liberties.
I'm concerned with guilt.
The moment an outsider tinkers
with a topic for the purpose of
being timely
& informative (how?)
something problematic
is perpetualized
regardless of the intent.
Write what you know, asshole.
I'm speaking to myself
I want Stacy Mum to be Irish.
I want her to be from Cork, Ireland.
I want Stacy to be in a psychobilly
noise band called
Post-Mortem Dance Fever.
I want Stacy to be a restroom muralist.
I want Stacy to do better than
Michael Quartz, honestly.
And she will, because she's a woman.
A strong woman who shouldn't rely on
or waste her time with a man whose concept
of time is skewed by his own permanence.
But, unfortunately, as the tossed schilling
whistles on its eternal descent into the Dammit Hole,
in order for it to count, to flay a significant cut,
he's got to fuck it up.
Because that's what
the white cis male feeds on.
And that isn't some kind of
self-hating propaganda.

Go ahead, ask any of my friends;
we fucking suck.

*   *   *

Stacy and Quartz are seated at a booth
in one of Seatown's oldest diners.
Stacy is playing w/ an ancient Tamagotchi
on her break from lyric writing.
Quartz is reading from his favorite book
Sayonara, Gangsters.
Stacy's Tamagotchi is damaged,
all it does is poop and die.
That's life, says Quartz.
How would you know, Stacy pfffffts.
Resentment is to be expected at this point.
Here is a man in his fifties,
who doesn't look a day past thirty,
who cannot fucking die,
and how does he choose to utilize
his abilities?
One failed attempt at suicide after the other.
At his leisure he slips in and out of the Living End and
the Dead Space like it's no thing.
It's no thing for him to unplug.
Without a single thought of how his actions have
scarred those around him, he flatlines
and sinks.
He swims into the angelic arms of Lady
Deathfingers, embalmed in a quiet shade of night
while the world quakes
in a collective torrent of anxiety.
Where will I be when the bomb drops?
There isn't a morning a headline
doesn't halt Stacy's thumb from scrolling.
Be it Neanderthal legislation.
Be it the bellicose rhetoric of a tyrant.
Be it pipelines through sovereign land.

Be it another mass shooting.
Be it another black life they say didn't matter.
Be it another rape victim dismissed,
discredited.
Be it another LGBTQ youth made invisible.
Be it the war on PC.
Be it random, isolated incidents of people
gone mad—Michael Quartz is exempt.
Michael Quartz does nothing.
It's not that he doesn't care,
he's just too self-involved to participate.
Marches cause intense flares of paranoia.
Every laugh is a laugh in his direction.
Every resting scowl is an overtly conscious mark
of disapproval.
These people can sense there's something...
there's something wrong with me.
Quartz *feels* for the mortals.
Quartz *hurts* for the mortals.
I am with you, says the banner.
But he can't be bothered.
His sense of humor and standards for decency
have shaped with the times, but he's by no means
progressive.
He *used* to make those jokes.
He *used* to practice misogyny.
And now he's stopped.
Quartz is angry and sad at the exact time he
should be so what more could we expect?
What do you suppose I do, he asks.
What will be my claim to fame?
This isn't about you getting a Wikipedia page,
Stacy says.
You're no-one's idea of a savior.
Deja Vu is a thick oil in the air.
She's said all this before.
The waitress returns with their orders.
Michael scoffs.

You've got to be kidding me, he tries to
communicate telepathically to the
waitress.
I asked for sweet potato curlies
not fucking JOJOS!

*　　　*　　　*

X. Ikaroa is the sole proprietor
of the Trappist Grant; a bi-annual
wish machine.
They scan millions of applications
from anywhere between
women dying of cancer who've resorted
to the mystical when modern
medicine has failed them,
to Hillbilly scum petitioning to
bring the General Lee back to TV Land's
regularly scheduled programming.
X. Ikaroa will grant any wish:
They will raise your Grandfather
from the dead.
They will cast a spell on the person
you love & make that shit reciprocated.
They will grant you an infinite amount
of wishes
& make you rich beyond your
wildest dreams—
as long as your pitch is well written,
detailed, and entertaining AF—
with bullet points.
X. Ikaroa especially enjoys
the absurd, the surreal—and twists!

*　　　*　　　*

One breezy, sun dappled
afternoon in April,

X. Ikaroa is scanning
the slush of Trappist applicants
with his beady, glaucous loupes.
They lift the brim of their silver pork pie hat
to wipe the slick of sweat
from their antennae-bangs,
wiggling vigorously like diced, nubby tentacles.
Golden rays of light pale the teal
bioluminescence of their skin.
The peculiar djinn turns rigidly from
one stack of applicants to the next
in a Burroughs-esque fashion,
when they stumble across a familiar name.
Edmund Quartz,
X. Ikaroa inquires silently.
No, this is Michael Quartz,
Edmund's son.
Astonished by this new discovery,
X. Ikaroa is filled with emotions of nostalgia
& a seed of nepotism is firmly planted.

    *   *   *

It is estimated that over five-
thousand planes are stuck in the air.
Not flying, not falling,
but stuck in place
like a broken crib mobile,
dangling at altitudes as high
as forty thousand feet above us.
They've been up there—
completely unseized by wind or gravity—
for nearly two weeks.
None of the pilots can figure out
how to get them to land.
Some passengers of these aircrafts
have gone as far as unhatching the overwing
exits to parachute back down

w/ unrivaled leaps of faith.
However, each attempt has been unsuccessful.
Flocks of people are walking on thin air,
treading clouds and suspended lakes
made of rainwater, limited
in its descent.
With your binoculars,
you can plainly see the sky is peppered
with these poor souls
clamoring down at us,
unable to touch their feet to the ground.
Reports have been made of people snatching
birds mid-flight,
as they are not affected by the phenomena.
Light tormenting strokes of feathery entrails
dress our once great, poetry
inspiring heights with fearful,
spasm conduction.
You can see miles of ocean,
swaths of rafts with desperate faces
whose arms have warped to jelly
from rowing their oars w/ zero gains to shore,
lost at a most magnificent
and surreal sea that refuses to carry them
in any direction but afloat.
Gun triggers have jammed,
knives won't stab,
cars won't start,
wheels won't turn—
civilization as we know it has
entered a dystopian era of stunted
proportions.
It's a beautifully tragic end
for the human race, in my opinion,
X. Ikaroa said, as they fidgeted with a tag
of paint peeling from the front door.
X. Ikaroa fed the coiled piece of paint
to their mouth and chewed it rapidly.

A disgusted frown soon overtook their veiny,
embryonic visage.
Brilliant even.
Quartz may have had good intentions,
but he was still holding the world hostage.
Freeze all man-made progress
until everyone gets along,
He wished.
Yup, it's that easy.
Nothing nuanced about it.
So simple!
Gross.
You couldn't have just wished for world peace
instead and bypass all the chaos and hysteria?
Stacy asked, tilting her head.
Where's the fun in that? X. Ikaroa jeered.
I don't know about you, but I'm a fiend for the
'will they prevail or won't they prevail'!
Do you have any idea what you two idiots have done!?
Stacy screamed, so irate she almost
vibrated off the porch.
Relax, said Quartz.
Everything
is going
to be
O.K.

*   *   *

Everything was not O.K.
& everyone did not get along.
But, they did come to one agreement:
Quartz must pay.
Since the people could not commandeer
a firing squad,
or behead him w/ blade
or inject him by needle
or tame the wildness of the flame

to burn him at the stake
and so on, and so on,
they opted for strangulation
& hanged his remains
from the giant Tylecodon
in the feeding grounds of
the ravenous Snub-
nosed Shug.
Each dawn he'd return
to the Living End,
the people would scratch their heads,
wait for dusk,
& string him back up again.
Centuries double like rust & moss
on the Catskills;
day light is clipped;
an inhaled, whooshless breath.
& w/ the tiding of night
comes the Snub-nosed Shug
in nocturnal pursuit;
ravenous &
whimpering as it yearns
for meat—
the meat screams, pleading
I'm a nice guy!

Part III | Armillaria

One cloud, one day
Came as a shadow in my life
And then left, and came back again; and stayed
Alfred Starr Hamilton

On the evening of the inauguration
I was eating two large slices
of pepperoni pizza on top of a trash bin
outside of Biggie M's on Capitol Hill.
In a matter of a few
minutes, I scarfed them down
to the very last fold of chewy crust
& swallowed.
Suddenly, as either a symptom
of an oncoming flu, alcohol poisoning,
or my body's natural response to DT's presidency,
a red hot aggravation swelled
inside my belly.
With the pressure building
and having been fully aware
I could not contain the eruption,
I broke apart from my group of friends
and walked to the other side
of the row of trash bins
and, thanks to my years of experience,
purged as though it was as casual
as feeding pigeons in the park.
For the next eight hours I purged.
Nothing I ingested would settle peacefully.
I purged every glass of water.
I purged every measly second of sleep.
I purged every profound instance of clarity.
The grit of my existentialism
made an indentation across my knees
as I gripped the porcelain waist
of the toilet bowl.

I half wept in a state of remorse,
having missed the Women's March.
Not because I was missing out
on a historic event, but because
I had published poems and posted rants
addressing my unrest,
yet I wasn't doing my part.
In what way had I ever effectively assisted
in the resistance?
Feeling outrage to the point of suffocating
myself with the shower curtain
does nothing.
Complaining to my wife
in the safety of our bedroom
does nothing.
Deleting my father for the pride
he takes in sharing deplorable memes
does nothing.
I thought, what will be my excuse
the day of the next rally?
Or if things, by some miracle,
do not get exponentially worse,
how will I provide my support
to ensure it improves,
rather than simply clicking "like"
staring into the popcorn void of the ceiling,
pondering as the years go by
like some kind of modern day
Rip Van Winkle.
The following Sunday I was standing
in the kitchen with my wife and her cousin
who was sitting on the counter
drinking from a can of cider.
She'd told me our old friend Sitka
had recently killed herself in New York.
She had moved there to attend law school.
The news knocked the wind out of me.
She wasn't a person I was particularly

close to, but I enjoyed her company
immensely in the past.
Sitka was hardcore.
She was the girl they'd escort
out of a bowling alley for lifting
her leg up,
spraying pee all over a urinal
in the men's restroom.
I saw her once at a metal show,
in heels sharp as fire pokers,
kick this guy she was dating straight
in the ribcage.
I had always admired her
tenacity, and now she was gone.
Like Ben, Aiden, Samantha,
and Frankie before her;
she was gone.
People who, I believe,
would've taken to the streets
a method of protest more impactful
than vomiting in the fetal position
until everything goes spotty and white.
They are gone, but I am here.
I have to have more than words.

*   *   *

I clock-out of my receptionist position
and leave the Met Park East Tower
in Denny Triangle
at around 5:30 PM to rendezvous
with Jay at Seatown's Red Deli.
He was visiting from Oakland
and only in town for the week
to release his second chapbook.
He may have invited me to read
at the event, but we didn't
have much opportunity to catch up,

so we penciled in some time
for us to grub on sandwiches and chat.
I was looking for non-
alcoholic beverages
when the waitress stopped by our table
to grab our drink orders.
all of our drinks are on the front page
of the menu, she said.
This wasn't correct.
All of the *alcoholic* drinks were
on the front page of the menu.
It was like,
No, no! You want theeeese drinks.
She didn't do anything wrong, though.
She was being helpful.
The majority of people on Capitol Hill
are always looking for
~ the boozy juice ~
and I'm usually one of them,
but not anymore (right now).
It had been a month and a half since
I had any booze,
which is the longest I'd been
sober in nearly five years.
I'll have a ginger beer, I said.
Jay ordered a cocktail.
There's usually some heavy
disaster or altercation
linked to every one of my quests
for sobriety,
so I'm prepared for Jay to ask
What happened?
I not only single-handedly ruined
my wife's first birthday since the wedding,
I fucking decimated the shit out of it.
My emotions ran so hot,
I even threatened to kill myself
over something miniscule

that I completely misconstrued.
Holy shit, man, Jay says.
does this happen often?
It's something I've battled with
my whole life.
Occurrences are few and far
between these days,
but it still happens.
Drinking definitely makes it worse.
See, every intelligent person I know
suffers from that, Jay said.
And I don't know what to do with his comment
because I've never felt like an intelligent person.
I've felt equipped with a privilege of having witnessed
and experienced what the underbelly
of the Dammit Hole has to offer—
which has left with me a with a quote/unquote
second sense—
but I'd never categorize myself as someone
who is either inherently intelligent or otherwise.
We'll save it for the Ego Books
when it's time to publish.
Sobriety comes with many positives, for sure.
I've lost some weight in the face and gut.
I look familiar in my reflection again,
which is nice.
I'm not living paycheck-to-paycheck
since cutting drinking from my budget,
which is also nice.
I do feel somewhat indifferent, though.
And when I don't feel indifferent,
I'm suddenly extremely irritable.
There's also a speed attributed to constant,
unsauced thought I have yet been able to
manage or cope with.
It's a high concentrate and
I haven't built a tolerance.
I miss the dreamy lucidity;

the romance w/ simple,
languid movements.
How music and even the slightest
wafts of inspiration
pulse.
I don't miss the dark shit.
I don't miss "the little triggers".
I don't miss the high-pitched ebullience of
a stalking, volatile, emotional breakdown
that will escalate with me standing over the edge
of a freeway overpass
or burning scrambled pigmentations into my flesh
with cigarette butts or knives
heated by stovetop.
I don't know why it took me this long,
but I couldn't have quit at a better time.
Why's that? Jay asked.
I told him about my wife's recent
diagnosis.
Chiari Malformation
is a neurological disorder where
the cerebellar tonsils
descend out of the skull
into the spinal area.
This results in compression
of parts of the brain and spinal cord,
and disrupts the normal flow of
cerebrospinal fluid (a clear fluid which bathes
the brain and spinal cord).
As partially quoted from
ConquerChiari.org
Symptoms include:
dizziness
muscle weakness
numbness
vision problems
headaches
problems with balance

and coordination.
When you're diagnosed w/ something
like that, you can't resist
doing your own online research.
Sure, we've read about all the people
that have lived with their symptoms
and have lead perfectly normal lives.
But then you come across
the people whose symptoms have increased
after the highly invasive surgery;
the fatalities;
the stories in which people have died
from sneezing,
in their sleep,
or warned not to laugh.
The Chiari diagnosis on top
of her lupus condition must
leave my wife with a disposition
so dismal I cannot possibly fathom.
That's why my timing couldn't
have been better.
She needs me clear-headed.
She needs her partner.
After we ate our sandwiches,
Jay and I decided to part ways
at the corner
of E Pine and Harvard Ave
as it was a convenient place for me
to catch my bus back to
Green Lake.
I felt guilty for monopolizing the conversation
w/ so much negative talk,
especially considering it may be
another year or so before we meet again,
but that's usually how one-on-ones generally go
when time has occupied the plate –
the pace of the seesaw is going to be interrupted
by a moment of stark insight or trauma

dying to be shared.
Dazzling, Jay said,
in reference to the sun setting
on the west,
sparkling through tree leaf
& ricochet.
Dazzling, I mock him.
Jay and I hug.
We briefly touch on travel plans
to Oakland
or somewhere in the middle
or no place ever.

*　　*　　*

Not every aspect of my life
is a performance.
The prose doesn't actively sweep
granules of chipped nickel
or bits of craggy rock
from beneath the rug
so I may appeal to an audience
or mainline catharsis,
but it is important to maintain
accountability and, sometimes,
to do so, I must
put myself in a vulnerable position.
First, I create an open space for dialog,
in case any friends have an opinion
in regards to my turning into a puddle.
I message them individually;
they have to know I'm *aware.*
We must stave from apathy
and learn that these "explanations" –
the why, and how –
are just elaborate excuses at this point.
As a means to feel the pure gravity
of what transpired,

I resort to another dislocation;
the pariah,
the villain –
Bacchanalia Fryspunkt.

*   *   *

All Ziv Devi wanted for her birthday
was a bouquet of white & pink
pastel balloons, opaque
& brimming w/ helium;
champagne and adoration;
cheesecake and surprises;
ModCloth & Dear Creatures;
to be engulfed in candelabra
sweetness.
She wanted flowers
in the sock drawer, flowers
hidden between book pages, flowers
folded into paper hearts
inscribed w/ kitty grammar
& maybe a gift card for luv waffles
& Americano she can buy
in the morning
on her way to the community clinic
where she works as a mental
health professional.
It seems like a lot when
broken down,
but life as a Quartz isn't easy
and, well, it's her fucking Birthday.
If Stassi Schroeder can make
the world stop for her,
so can Ziv Devi.
But, because it is her Birthday,
Her ex-partner Bacchanalia
Fryspunkt
is a puddle of quagmires,

sharpening a boning knife,
threatening
to slice the wrists of the nice boy
she just married nine months ago
whom Bacchanalia couldn't keep
herself
from possessing.
She obsessively hooks her demon claws
into the souls of the people Ziv loves,
the people closest to her,
and rips their souls out.
She drives their bodies into calamity
to hurt Ziv for not loving her back
unconditionally.
Fryspunkt trolls her by text,
I hope you enjoy the fucking cadaver!
Cut, cut, cut!
Ziv is sobbing at the ruin of the night
and the potential death of her husband.
Her Bobby.
She should have known it was
Fryspunkt
when she watched her husband guzzle
twelve pitchers of Guinness.
She should have known it was
Fryspunkt
When she watched her husband throw
a punch at a stranger at the club
and miss—breaking the crystal
of the Ted Baker watch she had bought him.
She should have known it was
Fryspunkt
when her husband left for Hotel Monaco
without her.
She should have known it was
Fryspunkt
when the pupil of his right eye
split and parted like in vitro

gone awry.
All Ziv wanted was for a day
where she could step away
from the pressure, wrap herself
in something warm and safe.
This is what she gets
for falling in love
in the Dammit Hole.

*   *   *

What if all the while you've been
using Becky as a scapegoat,
in all actuality – as though you're
caught in some cyclical
borderline pattern – you've been dating
shitty alcoholic white
guys with suicidal ideation,
consecutively.
Like, they're not really
possessed by a sadistic,
love struck demon from
the Dammit Hole—
they just suck.
Everybody needs a Pony;
someone raw
who's not afraid to call you out
on your shit.
Pony is Ziv's younger sister.
She says this to Ziv while
she longingly ponders the contents
of the envelope with her name on it,
propped against a bottle of champagne
resting in a bucket of lukewarm water
on the dresser next to the flat screen TV
in what was supposed to be the hotel room
her husband had rented for her birthday.
Pony casually says this to her

not ten feet
from the slashed to bits corpse Ziv used
to call her husband.
The splatters of blood on the perfectly
curated artwork hanging on the walls
appear aggressive themselves;
stab marks on stab marks
all around.
For example, Pony continues.
She withdraws two cans of green stuff
from the dead husband's old grey satchel
on the loveseat by the window overlooking
overpasses
overlapping overpasses
and office windows reflecting adjacent
hotel windows reflecting blue sky.
The sisters slurp together.
If we rummage through the banks
of your relationships before
our beloved Bacchanalia,
we will find that ogre
piece of shit Stuhać.
Here's a guy who'd come home
blacked out and literally rip
your limbs off. The next
morning he'd wake up with a
massive hangover to a spotless
apartment and you making coffee—
with your limbs still attached!
And he'd never think twice!
This behavior...
It went on for four years, Ziv!
You weren't there, Pony!
Ziv screams, her teeth graze
the bump of Pony's little nose.
The sisters slurp some more.
Bacchanalia is real.
Of all people, I'd expect

you to believe me.
Come on, Pony says,
I'm only checking in with you.
Pony's port-wine stain runs down the left
side of her face in rapids of plum.
She thinks this, matched with everything else,
gives her character an edge over Ziv;
the way in which she wears it.
As if somehow all she's overcome
makes her an expert on pain
& she holds the patent.
Ziv can't take it.
Not when her husband
is carved up and falling apart
like a loaf of dried tofurky.
If she didn't know the
sheets were supposed to be white,
she'd swear…

*   *   *

Haunted by second guessing
whether the bus driver watching
Ziv take her seat from the rearview mirror;
the neighbor who stalls the elevator;
the catcalling motorist;
the catcalling construction worker;
the cashier ringing up her groceries;
the bagger separating the raw hamburger meat
from the collard greens and chard;
the sudden stranger at the turning of a corner;
the hornet caught between the glass and the screen;
is possessed by Bacchanalia
or just a creep.
She looks into their eyes, she looks
for the doubling.
When will she reveal herself next?
When will she grace Ziv w/ another

performance?
The lid of her to-go cup
comes undone;
she spills coffee on her dress.
A sweet voice calls out to the barista
for a napkin.
Ziv looks into their eyes, she looks
for the doubling.

*   *   *

Bacchanalia sleeps in her jade
sarcophagus;
her consciousness presumably
miles from this cobweb grotto
hacking another body
so she may taunt Ziv
and punish Ziv
with no regard for anything
but her own entertainment.
Pony and Ziv push the lid just enough
for the light of their torches to illuminate
a flickering texture—
Bacchanalia's true form.
It is then she is reminded
of how much she has missed Bacchanalia.
The pain of the cavity is explosive;
it explodes.
She is such a beautiful and refractive
beryl.
She is swept,
She is swept again.
The memory has been repaired by
Bacchanalia's true image
& all Ziv desires now is to go back,
back to the Dammit Hole
& play the role of the person she wants to be
when she is with Bacchanalia.

Pony readies the jackhammer
to break Ziv's beloved rock;
her beloved Bacchanalia.
No! Screams Ziv.
No! No! No!
The tears are rising from depths
so deep she can barely breathe.
No! She screams.
No! No! No!
But it is too late.
Her love is sand.
Her love is dust.
Pony switches off the machine
and asks Ziv what is going on.
How did we get here, she says.
Pony doesn't know.
She doesn't know
what she has done.

*   *   *

Obviously I wasn't possessed
by some evil, butthurt demon
from another dimension
& my wife has never been in an abusive
relationship with a creature in
Serbian mythology.
The fantasy has been implemented
to better immerse myself
in the trouble I've caused.
I want to believe I've made up
for my behavior,
but only time will tell.
With drinking out of the picture,
I've snapped back to the quiet and awkward
persona.
I do good husband things like
take little trips to Lush and buy bathbombs

shaped like macarons
and offer to take the dog out to potty
in the morning so my wife can sleep in.
We're laughing again,
in spite of our worsts and in spite of this
new diagnosis and in spite of the possibility
of surgery.
My wife has been listening to the new
Mount Eerie record.
She also just finished watching
13 Reasons Why,
so the timeliness of the content
matched with our current situation
is impeccable.
At night—
after having scooped her from
the floor of our apartment
because a blinding light had appeared to her
without any source & dropped
her to her knees—
in the crook of my cradling her,
she turns to me and asks,
What will you do if that happens to me?
What will you do?
And I don't know.
I really don't know.

Part IV | Ghost Orchids

Believe in it? I've seen it done:
The gradual baptism of the moon
Before our eyes in oceanic light,
The sign of an eventual confirmation
When moonlight will become a general condition

Like love or the imagination – not only seen
But known, a phosphorescent tide in life and limb
The breathing bosom of the starry night,
The splendour and communion of the scene
A sea of fire in which we naked swim.
Daryl Hine

My Mother was chopping carrots and celery in the kitchen of our ground level two-bedroom apartment when she broke the news to me:

Have you heard the good news, she said.

Eyes gone white with the Holy Spirit

Did you know at any moment sentient earthquakes are going to murder all your friends?

Massive vacuumous holes are going to open up at various points across the globe, devouring their sin marrow

bones.

Then we can finally have some peace around here, she said.

Docile puma and lion will lay to rest underneath the baobab.

We will share vines of ripened fruit with Filipino children.
Sing in tongues. Oh, eternal joy & spotless

sun.

God's Love then hissed from behind the bushes near the sliding glass patio door.

God's Love trickled down the walls like a black maleficent tumor, flanking me at every turn—

an all consuming

       bog.

Embrace the maelstrom, she said. *If you're pure of heart, it should only tickle.*

      *   *   *

Our first lesson would lead us to a beach where we gingerly reviewed passages from within the book of Psalms.

We quoted in unison:

> *That men may know that thou,*
> *whose name alone is JEHOVAH,*
> *art the most high over all the earth*

I saw grids cut across the sky, cut across the sand,
the waves,   grey,

       saturated in tears;

I saw tiny grids calcify beneath
the skin on my hands,

the topography of creation,
netted—

we both nodded, *yes.*

*   *   *

A muzzle of palms yield simple,   kind civilities.

                              She's a ghost in the organization,
no one can see her;

                    my mother, the bent light

          bows her head, kneels,

                    she plays dead for them. The crowds

                    graze her afterimage

& she flickers a little,

          flickers to being elsewhere

with Honolulu blues & greens.

          A meeting place

                              where the pearl sky

                    opens.

*   *   *

Ghost orchids float like paper lumières
on the black waters of the black beach.
I mistake the preying Dendrophylax
for radiant
silken mantis.
I watch them slide back and forth
atop the longitudinal waves;
to and fro,
to and fro.

I am surrounded by moonlight
& phosphorescent dream rock
orbiting the island.
The elders
w/ their horseshoes and liver spots
have morphed into lumps of charred cedar.
Their once terminally-positioned teeth
scatter the grains of onyx
like the remnants of mollusks.
I thank them for helping me
expand my imagination.
Above my head, a shuriken whirs,
powered by telekinesis.
A second pair of hands have emerged.
I am a tarantula in a shadowplay.
I have giant hands for wings—
they grab the wind; I glide, flat
palmed.
They grab the waves;
the waves tug back. To rest
I bury my grey, ashen feet,
sprinkled with the sparkle of purple
salt,
into the grains of onyx
& when you have done this,
when you have drank the air,
your kiss, agape,
the Arbiters of the Living End
become arbitrary.
You can finally hear the voice of bliss,
& it is so quiet, so peaceful
when it speaks.
The Arbiters however have not disbanded
completely.
The Arbiters plan to return with a fierce
motivation,
adumbrated by the shrill of eels
in the blackened overcast;

like wight yaws
from the haunted stone-ender
from horrors, immemorial,
they will tangle you,
lash you w/ verisimilitude;
stark, encompassing traumas.
Deep-seated traumas.

My own voice doesn't even make a sound.
It is so quiet when it screams.

Ghost orchids float like paper lumieres
on the black waters of the black beach.
I trace the glow, I trace the sway of their
radiance for but a moment.
I cocoon myself with the clasping fingers
of my giant hand-wings.
Better darkness,
better sleep.
Better darkness,
better sleep.

> *Straddling each a dolphin's back*
> *And steadied by a fin,*
> *Those Innocents re-live their death,*
> *Their wounds open again.*
> W.B. Yeats

There are some new people in this room—I think—who need to understand—I think—that you can remove all the toxic friendships you want; get a haircut; spruce up your wardrobe; snap an attractive selfie; seek an alternative career path; ground yourself via procreation and marriage; move twenty-thousand miles east; go to therapy; go to meetings every day; run at dawn; stop listening to sad music; convert to veganism and Christianity; discover a hidden talent in the visual arts and never taste a single drop of alcohol in your life ever again—and you're still going to be you. Whatever ails or haunts you, whether it's a series of crap that hit you so fast you never learned how to cope, or it's one single traumatic incident in which you were the victim, perpetrator, or both; you need to recognize and come to terms with the fact that there's no erasure. One day you're going to be in the produce section of the grocery store snagging a pack of baby portobello mushrooms and then bam! And it's not like anything triggered you, either. Memories just circulate like that, man! I guess—I think—what I'm trying to articulate here is that you're always going to be the open flame. From here on out you have to be alert to yourself and the surroundings you engage. Burn bright for as long as you can and stay clear of explosive materials. Oh, and get over your aversion to clichés, that will also help.

The eloquent, Hard Knox wisdom of the egg shaped young man in the Green Bay Packers pullover remained unappreciated among the entirety of the group, sipping coffee. He smelled of gas pump and piroshky and a need to coach. But we didn't come here for that. We came here thirsty for the anecdotes of society's scorned and lovelorn fuck ups. We want to compare atrocities and connect through our shared experiences so that we may feel a little less alien in our attempts to stay conscious, not to hear another ignorant rant concerning the inexistence of time travel. It's difficult to listen intently and not be distracted by my own inner monologue while I rehearse in preparation of my turn at the podium in the throes of someone else's turn at the podium. Like, that's what we're all doing here. We're either just waiting for our turn to speak or cynically picking apart the person already talking.

It's funny, all the people in my life who make fun of me for not having a license have had their licenses revoked for Driving Under the Influence. I tell them what's going on with me and all they do is talk down to me. You don't have to stop drinking, they say. You need be more mature and handle your liquor better is all. Handle my liquor better!? I'm fucking thirty! I've been doing this shit for fifteen years! That's the problem, there's no escape. This mentality is everywhere.

And it goes on like this for a while as we circle around the room. If you don't have a papa bear rubbing your shoulders with some bullshit dogma about accountability you've got another guy complaining that the drunks he's hung out with his whole life are—SURPRISE—still drunks! It's a cult inside and outside.

But then someone… This woman—a young woman whom I could only best describe as the molecularization of Ziggy Stardust and Sun Ra's music—took to the podium.

Hiya! My name is Niamh (pronounced "Neve" like "Steve") Tutoula, and not only do I have a name comprising Irish and Nigerian roots, I am also an alcoholic from the future! Lucky me, I was born above Seatown in the suspended waters of Lake Amazon Prime where I was punched from my mother's embrace by a bolt of lightning! Does this make me some kind of demi-goddess? Who knows!? Somehow I survived the electric discord and landed in the Woodlands, west of the Concrete Troll. There, I was raised by Ciao the Red Panda—he taught me martial arts! I can see by the look on your faces a question formulating the likes of 'why would someone traveling from the future choose to make a pit stop at an AA Meeting'? Well, that's a loaded question, really. The mission. The pressure. The history behind me. The fate ahead of me.

I keep telling myself my actions have served the best interests of the Living End, yet I'm still shaking. My thoughts won't stop racing on this track of remorse. They're spiraling now into darker territories; uncomfortable domains of buried, gritty shit. My eyes are puffy and bloodshot from sleepless nights filled with intense, paroxysms of screaming for oblivion. All I want is to suck on some tequila and stomp my feet, shake my ass, and fuck, fuck, fuck until I'm too tired to even eat a pizza. But let's not kid, I'm eating that fucking pizza.

I was outnumbered eight-to-one.

The Secret Servicemen emerged from the parking garage beneath the high-rise of condos in downtown SEA. Four men lead the way while another four followed behind, carrying President Revok's palanquin and—within it—President Revok. President Revok peered out through the curtains of the palanquin and dumped a receptacle full of candy wrappers, littering the blood-rusted streets. Rage consumed me the moment I saw him. I was reminded of the pain of my great, great uncle Xander Pluto and how the president's rhetoric plagued his mind. I was reminded of the images of police brutality. What it must've been like in the age of the Alt-Right Edge Lords. . . I can tell you now it never ceases. If only I could travel farther back.

Out of habit, the first dead man withdrew his pistol to shoot me as I sprinted towards him, but of course it jammed. I impaled him with a flying kick that cut right through his chest.

The second and third dead men's tongues swelled; their lips turned blueberry blue as I choked them simultaneously.

The fourth dead man hit my arms as hard as he could in an attempt to loosen my grip from their throats. When their bodies fell limp, I leaped onto the fourth man's shoulders and snapped his neck like a raw spaghetti noodle between my thighs.

The fifth, sixth, seventh, and eighth dead man lowered the palanquin gently and circled around me. In the blink of an eye, my hardened fists drummed their jaws clean off. Globs of blood dribbled and spatter-blushed upon their white dress shirts. Broken aviators everywhere.

President Revok had nowhere to run to. I could hear him hyperventilating with fear behind the curtains of the palanquin.

I ripped a piece of curtain from the palanquin and tied it around his neck and dragged him out onto the blood-rusted streets now littered with candy wrappers. I stood on his spine and pulled at the piece of torn curtain, strangling him. It didn't take long before he was depleted of all signs of struggle and life.

I waited for awhile, half expecting oxygen to return to him; wondering if he, like me, had a little bit of Quartz in him, as surely no monster has ever died so easily.

No one clapped.
No one clapped because we knew her secret had to die with us.
So instead, we laughed.
And laughed.
We laughed as we've always laughed.

Manifest Dynastes

You must be disgusted
But I need to keep writing because everything else is death
I'm self-sufficient, mad, endlessly producing
I don't need money, I just need your love
Or your approval, anything

Jenny Hval, Undressing Love

Ashwagandha : how to exacerbate the longing / Query the process / The breadth between muted tissue & initiated physicality / END interim / END pause / Roll credits / Frame your fodder / If you can not assign origin of responsibility / A thinking, pulsating wasteland of perineum / Gift ownership / It must be god / Your voice cords move them / Poached like tumbling die / The great Ruby Bermúdez in the sky / Drowned separate from you / BEYOND the suspended lakes / The 13yr old Puerto Rican child / Overseer of the Living End / Pierced to the turbine with space buns / Of black ravens and peonies / Ruby Cosplays Sailor Moon / Blood Moon they say / They're dressed in red skirt and red lapel and red mascara and perfect circles of red blush / It is Ruby's onus to audit the Living End / To comb its climate; politically, meteorologically / Etcetera, etcetera / Evulse, cleanse and sterilize / The unjust of man or any / Supernatural lacerations / When there is downtime / Ruby just wants to ebb & nap the fuck out / It is not Ruby's prerogative to influence or interfere with the occupants of the Living End / *Your handicaps are pure fabrications* / *When will you claim satisfaction, Noah* / They ask / *Drained of dream stuff* / *These incessant midnight prayers are all too distracting* / *Inconsiderate* / *You are a constant formulation of wants* / *It's always about you* / *Your name already bears success* / *Is it because it already bears this mysticism of success* / *You don't know how to measure* / *Fin or full* / *Is it metamorphosis you seek* / *The bleep, bloop, and blink of an 8-bit LVL UP* / *Totality of fire-breather vs. actinic keratosis* / *What will it take* / *What will you do* / *What will come of this pacification* / *Enlightenment caries* / *Kilesa Mara* / *Sorry* / *Not Sorry* / *I will cut every corner to shut you up* / *Slake the Dybbuk on my back* / *Shoo* / *Shoo* .

Getting booked to do a bunch of readings won't get you published /
Getting published frequently will not guarantee you a constant audi-
ence / You want to produce timeless content and receive the instant
gratification of effervescent recognition from your peers / What you
fail to admit you need is community, between the pages, penned
in the margins / A happy medium of the written and the spoken /
A life / Fledging / Affability / A radar for appropriate behavior and
demeanor and are you progressive enough / Noah Fang Quicksilver
/ Convey something / Seek out positions with power / Assume a role
in leadership / Host your own / Recurrent sorbet / Set yourself apart
from the others / Appropriate their genres / Pillage and plague their
spaces / Draw your bridges for them / Lure them in / They will have
nowhere else to turn to / They will look up into the sky and be met
with resounding liquefaction / You have been blessed with the egg /
Incubation nears completion / Use what Ruby gave you / This is how
we achieve our greatness, Noah / Schadenfreud hour / We shall benefit
from the coming phenomenon .

Go to the Cerise Gallery / Order two bags of popcorn with pink salt /
Take a seat at the table with Durian Gaffney / Talk shop / You met him
at the Guy Who Dances With Women Made of Coat Hangers' show
/ Since then he's introduced you to a plethora of local like-minded
talent / A sect of rising pseudointellectuals / The No St. Poets / Duri-
an is Legendary / The founder and curator of the now defunct Happy
Corpse Reading Series / He is older than you / But not by much / Dis-
tinguished by grimace and gray / Well versed in the trials and tribu-
lations of name making / He is like you / As much as he enjoys litera-
ture he finds straight readings dull / No matter who the feature / His
mind trails off and sometimes he gets lost / Forgetting to drop kernels
[extending cognition] to follow back home / He is an innovator / A
man with ideas / A little black book with names near and far / Pick his
brain / Squeeze it like a loofah full of suds / Scrounge up all the genius
you can / *Every night there is a literary happening / Happening here at
the Cerise or somewhere else / Do the cliques co-mingle / Not a chance /
We're all stuck here together / Strangers together / That's where we come
in, Noah / We're going to give them a new original series / A nexus for all
schools / It will be challenging behind the scenes but it will be simple in
its execution / When was the last time we had a touring poet in this city /
Since before the curse / Back when planes flew / Back when automobiles
were mobile / This is a time for digital pilgrimage / I know people, Noah /
Poets from Ontario, Tokyo, and Lima / We can record them / Project their
images on the wall here / I mean fuck we already have the popcorn / We'll
get the Guy Who Dances With Women Made of Coat Hangers and his
band of art theater brats to perform / When starting something new you
have to ask yourself if it is unique and if it is relevant* / Before he is done
speaking you already know you are going to sacrifice him to the egg
/ *We'll call it COMING ATTRACTIONS / I am excited to work with you,
Noah*, he says / Clicking his tongue at a piece of kernel stuck between
his teeth .

We steep the egg in a cup of Durian / Percolation & pulp / Subtle shades of Durian's enigmatic mise en scene dye the fragile layers of calcium carbonate / Methods of curation seep through the micropylar regions / The egg is absorbing the schematics of the character's psyche and abilities / Of organization / Behold, Noah, divine administration / You have taken the first step toward achieving greatness / The cracks in the shell breathe in patterns of wisteria and now / The world as you know it / May finally be seen through the distortion of your own eyes

.

Part stalking regimen / Part tutorial : How to learn from your prey /
Mental camouflage for your modern day imposter / Titrate responsibly
/ Wednesdays look like Market Fresh / The Cerise Gallery's weekly
open mic / Hosted by Calluna / The strawberry blonde with dread-
locks, thinned and sparsely entwined / Thoracica lentigines / Peri-
orbital, barnacled sun spots / Another HOWL inspired degenerate /
Beats the drum / With the charisma of Moriarty / Chinaski in carnate
/ Wielding a bestial, feline glare / Encased in the shapeliness of an Ital-
ian vase / She riles the crowd / Swings from rafters / Kicks over ampli-
fiers / *Tonight you could die / You could die tonight / And there is no other
place / No place other than here / You should be / You rather be* / She is
the mother bird / Hovering o'er / We choke on her spit up / Our first
taste of the world / *This will sustain you* / She promises with the aura of
ordainment / What is this some kind of sermon / Maximum occupan-
cy is but a memory / Calluna has a magnetizing personality / Fun and
cool people are here / The Cerise is packed / Like stalks of bolting on-
ions / Shot up through concrete / You hate when your coordinates have
been compromised by the interference of other poets / You can sense
them among the crowd / Hoarding all the metaphysics / Of each object
/ Interaction / Privately rehearsing the material they've prepared for
the open mic / You are a radio that has been roomed with other radios
/ And the song you are playing feels like a hit / The most beautiful air
wave to flow through you / But no-one can hear it / I can't hear it / Not
with all these other stations playing / If I could enjoy its structure by
alternative means / Senses / My nose even / Olfactory white dances in
the tulips / They are sucking all of the thoughts that could be poems
out of the atmosphere / Here comes the amnesia of being / We get it
you hate other poets / Yet here they are / Fevered amateurs / Better,
worse, or unimpressive / Feeding on growth encouragement / Calluna
is one hell of an MC elettrificate / Something you could never be / You
could organize the damn thing but have you truly seen yourself / Own
the presentation / Harness the mission .

We were at the second-hand bookstore / Tunnel Books / I still remember the expression you made when you first used the word *clandestine* / You froze as though the messiah within you had peaked consciousness / Coaxed through language / Bewildered you froze like a sloth / Diving into a bank of cooling glass / That is the expression you are now making / Noah Fang Quicksilver / Your choice of word for that moment was not nearly as sensitive as the decision you're dealt with now / Anchor / Calluna is tied w coaxial cable / Her screams are contained by the mouth you've taped / You are thinking about those lips / What her kiss might be / The depth of a green apple / You are thinking about your first kiss / Shudder / You were five or six / Playing on the swing set with a spunky ginger / The little girl was curious to lend you a peck on the pucker and you lost it / You didn't give her permission / Because you didn't give her permission / And you remembered what happened / The last time you didn't give someone permission / Your first true lucid memory / And that's why you screamed at her / Sullied the innocence of the childish dare / And now the two events / Which have become memories / Correlate due to a symptom of trauma / All these things wrong with you / You can't even offer Calluna as sacrifice to your itty bitty instar grub / Without shaming yourself for fixating on how you're fixating on a pair of concealed lips / When you should be focusing on the banjo plucking beat poet you're about to feed to your itty bitty instar grub so you may absorb her powers of stage presence and hosting capabilities / Prayer is nonsense at this juncture / Stop it, Noah / Stop it / Our holy Ruby Bermúdez has blessed you with the only tool you need to succeed / They have given you the power / These prayers will only know the silence they are spoken in / Noah / Noah Fang Quicksilver / The egg has hatched and so have you / It is time to feed your instar .

Three months sober / I bet you wish you had had the foresight / Ten
years ago / Before getting a beer stein tattooed on your right calf /
Now that you're wearing shorts among the droves of local literati
decked out in neon Helvetica / How basic do you think you look RN
/ At Book Swamp / Of all places / The monthly book fair block party
organized by Neb Therill / Editor-in-chief of *LIGHTNING haus* / A
publishing outfit that prints four collections a year / Mostly by MFA
graduates more interested in pursuing a cameo appearance on Com-
edy Bang! Bang! / Neb Therill is the type of guy who will solicit work
directly from you and then reject your manuscript w a form letter /
IT'S A NO FROM ME, DAWG / You've invited Neb to read at a number
of events / Extraordinary IMO / But he's never invited you to read
at any of his / Interactions play back over and over / Anxiety's rigor
amplifies the slightest snicker / Inquisitive brow / Neb exudes an air
of prestige / Confidence lies / In the likelihood of his knowledge of
your shit talking / Bitter whispers / Pungent / CBD & THC help you
maintain the stride of a customer service representative merchandis-
ing an end cap / As you approach him / There are thousands of online
journals / An average of five or more readings a night / & Neb still
refuses to admit poetry has become cool / *No, it's a necessity* / He says
/ *Every person needs to eat but we're not all Michelin chefs* / There are so
many skinny white people in various vintage frames and thrift store
sweaters / Wool beanies / Smart denim from Pearl street / Perusing ta-
ble after table of enough small independent publishers to fill an entire
city block / But no / Poetry isn't cool / You see we need that academia
pomp / Indie elite / Neb, the purple flannel accountant / Looks at
you from behind a pair of fake-awake glasses / He is standing at the
LIGHTNING haus table on the sidewalk in front of the candy striped
entrance of the Cerise Gallery / You pretend to price check and make
mental note of the titles on display / Greetings happen / Noncom-
mittal small talk / You meander the perversion of self-promotion /
Tell him about the flood of publications you've been getting / Whet
the palate for the pitch / A pocket version of Book Swamp to coincide
w COMING ATTRACTIONS / You attempt to persuade him with
wholesomeness / It's about melding worlds in the poetry community

/ Or possibly mending broken connections / He doesn't bite / *I'm just SWAMPED,* he says / The pun is clearly intentional / All you can hear is / *IT'S A NO FROM ME, DAWG* / You play back the interactions over and over / You wonder if the answer might have been different had you invited him on social media instead / Under the guise of avatar / But it's no time for constructive let down / The instar is a growing grub / And he's about to get bigger .

You're picking at another inky carving / On your wrist the words / Epic in Holtzschue / Back when everything / Ironically was / You're such a ridiculous character / Outgrowing the need for stories / You want what comes NEXT / Book Swamp has ended / The crowd of stuffy buyers has dispersed to cantina row / Neb Therill is packing up his titles and heading home / Growling emits from your duffel bag / Your chubby baby instar is famished / Killer daddy / Take care of your underling / Tail him / Strike in the ensconcement of privacy / When all witnesses have diminished / Blinking bushes / A dog, barking / Neb drops a small saddle-stitched chapbook / He is only a short few conquerable feet ahead of you / As he bends over to pick up the chapbook that has fallen his fake-awake glasses drop from their perch / He is locked on one knee / Neb snores / Neb is asleep / Has he been like this the whole time / Sleep walking / Sleep editing / Sleep living / You push him over, unzip the instar / Let the feeding commence / Absorb the brevity of sharp wit and indie smugness / Academia pop / The sound of a ravenous insect chewing on intestines entices you to distract yourself w some light reading / The chapbook is titled *Evil Goes to Taco Bell* by Zakochany / Neb must've snagged it from a neighboring table at the book fair / It's a long poem / A suicide note by the Alaskan serial killer Israel Keyes reformed into a creepy love poem dedicated to Taco Bell / *Flaccid in my grip, gushing all that nacho cheese* / Intrigued / You dust off the scum of leaves & dirt / Could be refuse / And the cover is wet / W droplets of Neb Therill's blood / You leash up your burping, satisfied and sated instar / Killer Daddy / Your baby is a slippery unfurled accordion / Walk off into the sunset / A dog, barking .

Seven-hundred and twenty / Is the amount of friends you had / Before you posted the status / Celebrating a week of milestones / Three months of getting shamed by the bartender when asking for refills on ginger ale / Six years ago to the day / You were riding the clipper from SEA to B.C. when the curse had been enacted / The vessel's motor / Suppressed by a sorcerer's wrench / The laws of physics augmented / You couldn't physically get into the water / You had to walk on it / A squishy tarpaulin / Terrain of heckling whales / Mist yr face / Now you have seven-hundred and nineteen friends / Someone didn't approve of the sentimental #tbt / Whatever happened to actively supporting the people you know / Maybe they know too much / What do they know / How much do they know / You're getting sloppy, Noah / What you did to Neb was in broad day / Someone must've seen you sic the instar / Shaping want / That must be it / People aren't that petty / Are they / No matter / You've discovered a game changer / A new quintessential token for your development / It begins w the diorama of a dream / Durian Gaffney / A charismatic, energetic capital kicks the bottom out / Calluna / Polish the grime with shoegaze / Sharpen the cut of the knife / To align with the audience of Magnetic Fields and Portlandia / Imbibe in academia's pamplemousse / Neb Therill / At the zenith of your Everest you laugh madly at both the current definition of the world and the enigmatic void which dominoed your being / Chutes and cervix / What are the possibilities before word language / Googoo gaga > Mama > mumbo-jumbo > Dada > Then Gozo / Not gonzo / Reinvent the meaning of symbols / The timelapse of an echo / Reverberates in both directions / What happens when you fuse rebel w pro / Zakochany the spork / Neu Ancient / Holy Trinity / Holy theremin / Embodiment of Tesla spark / Of genius / You don't quite understand immediately but given the time to gestate. . ./ Like Bök's Xenotext / This is cognizant scheme skin / Far more violent of course / Your Little Shop of Horrors / Visible in laptop light / Is a pile of sweating white curds / Your instar pulses w blood lust / Transformation is nigh / Noah Fang Quicksilver / Prepare the fourth course / Zakochany béchamel .

Have you ever tried to lick the bathwater / w the shadow of your tongue /
Vapor squirts from Zakochany's ears when he spks / *I have outgrown*
word language / Oral and scribe / Straight poetry is for flat-earthers / And
every mythos has its limits / It isn't daring enough / My evolution as a poet
is nonlinear / The sounded wail appeals / Glottal crops / The genome of
feeling in the presence of a thimble / I owe my life to objects / More so than
the transition from one compartment to another / When I spin the wheels
on my skateboard / When I paw them w friction / It is a loaded symbol
is it not / You are reminded of the old order / What used to happen after
it touched the ground / When you embarked on the air above the asphalt
/ Catching scabs / The unexpected jolt of dragonfly / When we could get
angry at the need for patience / What our lives have become / Trapped in
the repetition of footfall / Feral capitalists / Gessoed in Dupieux & dross
/ Our conveniences have been usurped / In the new modern world / The
great asphyxiation of Aeolus / We must recognize that the very fact a curse
of this magnitude has been unleashed / Elucidates possibilities far more
valuable and beneficial than having the means to get somewhere faster / A
door has closed so a window may open / But the question is / Noah Fang
Quicksilver / Are we to exit through the now open window / Or wait to
befriend a vicious, entitled raccoon / That is my current project / You are
mesmerized / That's the flavor / This is too good to be true but yet it
is true / Your expressed fandom was hyperbolic bait but here you are
/ Sitting across from Zakochany AKA Neu Ancient / Listening to him
gloat about his past collaborations w the Ruefle Bot on Twitter / It is
hookah hour at the Cerise Gallery / The Cabinet of Dr. Caligari is pro-
jected on the wall / Insecurities jerk / You can't let go of the mystery
person who unfriended you / You went from having seven-hundred
and twenty friends to 719 / How incomplete / Who could it be / The
ex who is married w children / Nope, she's there / Coworker with
conflicting political and basic human rights beliefs / Nope, he's there /
Could it be Millicent Quartz/ She published you in *Tornado Summit* a
few years back / Perhaps she was offended by you removing the press
from your bio / Or shamelessly self-promoting yourself every time
you had a piece accepted / Maybe she hates your social media persona
/ Or maybe she thinks you're an awkward, problematic dick / OMG
it is her / Who publishes someone and then unfriends them / Is her

opinion of you circulating among the other publishers / Maybe she deactivated her account or had her previous account deleted and this is a new account you're looking at and she just didn't make the effort to seek you out and send you a friend request / Or maybe you're just garbage Noah / *So what's with the 'Fang'* / *Noah 'Fang' Quicksilver* / Zakochany asks you / Cringes happen / There's a story you're not proud of / It haunts you on good days and bad / You make up a biting fetish you never had to avoid talking about it / This sounds like an explanation he can stomach / Expectations painted Zakochany as tall and lanky / Shiny black hair / Not a stubby uncle fester in an Elizabethan collar / How are you going to convince him to come to your apartment / Your instar was too lardy to fit through the door / Let alone a duffel bag / If only you could've brought it with you / You tell him you forgot to bring your copy of 'Evil Loves Taco Bell' / You would appreciate nothing more than having him sign it / Especially considering it is the last remaining physical copy that exists documenting his coitus with word language / It is only a couple of blocks / Normally Zakochany would turn down the offer but he can't remember the last time he was invited to another person's home / It is only a couple of blocks / You won't even break a sweat / The instar is so enormous all you will have to do is open the door and push / Even his screams will be devoured / He will never see it coming .

Accretions of poetics bond like platelets / Enriched w various stylistic elements / You have your theme / You have your host / You have your poise and grandeur / You have your brush with abstract deliverance / The instar has shed its exoskeleton / COMING ATTRACTIONS ferments within the carapace / The shell of your pupae closed tightly / Sealing the incubation of an experimental hybrid / For the first time in your life / No one bailed / The featured performers have been reliable in sending their solicited recordings / The Man Who Dances With Women Made of Coat Hangers teases you w updates daily / 'Choreographed Klazo' he calls it / *If Jodorowsky was a minimalist. . ./* As the date approaches you come to realize you haven't run any promotions / You can't just build it, Noah / The line-up is fantastic but without promotion / You may as well be jacking off / Solo snowballing w a selfie / Cute pancake filter / Post flyers / Notify the press / Socialize [for profit] /

Tag tag tag tag tag tag tag tag tag tag tag tag tag

/Everyone and anyone who might have an inkling of interest / You've cultivated stage presence but you severely lack the knowledge of how to / As your old doctor once put it / *get belly buttons through the door* / Sit some asses down / Market your shit, Noah / Ruby Bermúdez / Our blessed auditor cosplaying in the sky / Did not risk the most coveted position in the Dammit Hole for nothing / It appears more blood must spill / Shepherd's blood / Baste the pupae w savvy marketing skills .

$5 cover / Whether you plan to sign up for the open mic or not / Proceeds go to the winner of the slam / Toward the Cerise Gallery's rent / It pays for renovations, upkeep, employee compensation / Etcetera / I know you don't care about any of that shit / & If you were still drinking and penniless [in theory] / I might understand your apprehension to contribute / But you're here to sniff out the feature / Jarrahdale Green / The entry fee will get you closer, Noah / Contribute / Sometimes they don't charge for sparkling water / Does it have to be sparkling / Icy penetration / The gnashing of teeth on foil / Your improprieties will not be disputed due to your inability to conduct conversation w strangers fluently / Keep calm / You don't have to be disingenuous or an extrovert to survive in this pit, Noah / Just don't tell them about the giant pupae / Blood sack / Back home / Or your plans for world domination & / You'll be alright / This event pulls a different demographic than Market Fresh / Which attracts the DIY anarchists, junkies, and musicians / It isn't stuffy with the floral embossed / Ephemeral swans like Book Swamp, either / It's street / Colloquial / There are *regular people* here / Dishwashers and landscapers and school counselors come here every Monday to show their welts / The calluses they've removed with the pumice stone / Through spoken word / It's a lot like country music in the sense that you either hate it or you love it / And no one really deviates from the formula / Everyone adheres to the same poet voice / Woke Brooklyn janitor / Delivering heart-rending / Tear jerking / Poems about social justice / Racism / Every brand of trauma / Overcoming adversity / Substance abuse / These are all very important things to touch on and there should definitely be a safe haven and you're totally onboard / Only you hate slam with a passion / The way they snap their fingers / The weird, appreciative *mmm* sounds their brains make in unison / It has a tendency to get way too real and sometimes when things get real they get cheesy / Sorry, but you're going to have to stomach through it / If you want to get to Jarrahdale Green / Why Jarrahdale Green, you ask / This is a man who built himself up from nothing / He never caught a single break / In and out of juvi / He later graduated to prison where he spent most of his young adult life / He owns a fry stand and works two part-time jobs to support three small children all on his own / He's a widower / Jarrahdale lost his wife in a mass shooting / Back when guns still worked / Because even before the curse bad things still happened to good people / Jarrahdale has VIPoma / A rare pancreatic tumor / It is terminal / Now that every form of transportation / Sans palanquin and piggyback / Has been dismantled / He does not have access to the healthcare he most desperately needs to hang on a little bit / A little bit longer / He does his best to provide / He saves every drop of money he earns from his performances on the side / From the poetry pamphlets he sells at each venue / Jarrahdale is active on Twitter / Facebook / Instagram / Everyone fucking knows Jarrahdale / Slam champ / You're here to observe / You're here to learn from the final master / It's not your fault if the roof caves in .

Let go / Let go of your guilt, Noah / Let go / I know it is much easier said than done / As it was / Your final prayer to Ruby Bermúdez / *Drop the roof on Jarrahdale / Here & Now / So I may glean the spirits of his best offerings & baste my pupae w a popular online persona / Tantalizing press packages / Sleek business cards / Kill two birds w one stone / Having the Cerise out of commission will lessen the threat of competition* / Ruby answered your prayers, Noah / Stop gazing into your reflection / Wet reflection / So pensive w remorse / I want elation / You've come so far, Noah / You've done it all / In just a few short moments the cocoon will molt anew / Shedding flakes of dried blood / Like coffee grounds / From cell to sand / Everything we've worked for / Everything we've stolen / Sprouting membranous wings / Olive-green elytra / Claws / Ginormous head and thoracic horns / Forming pliers / *To ply* / Magnificent Dynastes / Manifesting destiny / The date has been chosen / The public has been notified / Rejoice / Rejoice / Our demonic beetle / Living venue / Shall catapult you to celebrity / Or devour trying .

How . Is . This . Possible / The beetle stands on the rubble of le ole Cerise / *Cristo de la Concordia* / Between Tunnel Books and Vinyl Never Dies / Stanchions erect for Kali tragus / Misplaced crickets / Not a single person showed / Not anyone / Except for the Man Who Dances with Women Made of Coat Hangers / He is dancing with himself in the abdomen of the Dynastes / Drowning his disappointment in champagne / After everything we've done / It's all been done for naught / When you call Rhys / One of the No St. Poets who *promised* he'd be there / He tells you he can't hear you / He can't hear you over the band playing / What band / Where / *The fundraiser for the Cerise Gallery at Gasworks Park / Everyone's here* / Really, you say / IS FUCKING GOD THERE / *No, but Ruby Bermúdez is* / How . Is . This . Possible / Your sacrifices were on point / You managed to book some of the most talented up and coming poets from across the country and abroad / COMING ATTRACTIONS was voted #1 on the list of events to check out this wknd / It's a smorgasbord of ingenuity / There's a small press pop up book fair / A MAN WHO DANCES WITH WOMEN MADE OF COAT HANGERS / The event is inclusive to all genres and people / The venue is a GIANT BEETLE / Have I lead you astray, Noah / Noah Fang Quicksilver / Where did we go wrong ?

The Imposters

If my heart scowls now,
it is only because a certain epidermal contact with the enemy,
areally limited, has been postponed.

R. H. Barlow

PRETEXT

A rendezvous w syncope
near syncope

What isn't a damp, faint cry
of dumb twilight

Embrace the clammy
embrace

Soft crest of water
racing from the faucet

You've never felt more alive
cradled, anything but flesh-toned

An axolotl in a diaper
kind of euphoria

Haunting deflation
near deflation.

The fuzzy eyeball, nauseous
w invisible hives
feeling
is something I associate
with having to wake up
at an ungodly
hour
to go to the airport.

"An ungodly hour"
meaning it is too early,
even for the gods.
The gods are sleeping
while I put my socks on
& dry heave

simultaneously.
The gods are sleeping
while I splash the wall
in my throat
with cold water.

But I'm not going to the airport.

I'm doing the dishes,
& the gods are awake now.

I feel this way because I rebelled
against time
so that I may catch up
with the time I have lost,
time paid.

Watching Okja,
making comments to myself:

This South Korean girl
[Seo-Hyun Ahn]
is going to go places.

If Paul Dano is in it,
you know it is an instant
classic.

In order to add a little relevancy
to the mundanity of my life,
I sign up for a free month trial of
Hulu w/ Showtime.

And I'm proud to say,
people of the world,
I'm finally watching Twin Peaks: The Return.

And I can't simply enjoy,

it's imperative for me to share these updates.

Social media is harder to quit than smoking cigarettes.

I only want to smoke when I'm drunk and high on sociability
or distraught & sunken

in the syrup of the past.

How I've been hurt and how I've retaliated.

I am present in those moments
as though I'm inhaling the very oxygen
recycled by memory.

The room is spinning legs
over tongue.

Illusory extremities pull me
through the vivid interstices of traumatic environs.

In the kitchen I am tied to a tree
on Catalina Island. . .

But I haven't had a drink in six months.

The kitchen is just a kitchen and I haven't had a cigarette
since.

I want to be online right now.

Resign myself to the distractions of
my glowing algorithms.

A mask of liquid light.

The attempts to disconnect are real.

I've deactivated the account three times this week.

Changed the password to a complicated alphanumeric mash up

& I still can't keep away.

I want to keep away.

I believe, for some reason, unplugging
will ground me.

This is my yurt of tranquility.

But I need to know how the racist burger joint
will respond to the community's call-out and boycott.

Will they be accountable or will they first lie and then confess
with a list of
excuses--*they are victims of political correctness.*

I need to observe how the SJWs handle the Alt-Right trolls,
fanatically pushing the benefits of psilocybin.

Take notes.

I need validation.

If I post an image of an iguana
doing something un-iguana like
with the caption, *same*
it will garner ridiculous amts
of hearts and wows and ironic angry
reaction emojis.

But if I post a link to a recent poem
I have had published,
I'm lucky if that post
garners half the response.

It's based on the activities people associate you with.

Your state of presence in their lives
during said activities.

I'm known first for my iguanas,
so they like the iguanas.

If you haven't noticed, I'm severely self-centered.

I don't believe the methods in which I utilize social media
helps.

I even registered for a Twitter
& set all my tweets to private
to help curb cravings
like I've done with N/A beer
and electronic cigarettes.

But it isn't helping.

I can't stop.

I need to stop.

Important aspects of my history have risen through the soil
like a strange ink,
and they require my full, undivided scrutiny.

–

The Cutters is a city.

The Cutters is a city that runs purely on thaumaturgic energy.

The source of this energy comes from a man known to those of us in the Living End as Count Marco.

He wills the use of instruments made obsolete by Michael Quartz; a white male immortal with white male guilt whom made a wish in hopes for world peace, long ago.

The wish was granted by a sadistic genie named X. Ikaroa.

Together, they lanced the reactant properties of all man made weapons; from the assault rifle to the pointed stick.

Together, they seized engines, froze thy spokes.

We can't drive, we can't swim, we can't fly.

Little metallic dots of abandoned aircraft twinkle in the sunlight like intrusive stars.

Hunks of marine vehicles float in place, forever anchored.

Rusty eyesores.

We can only travel by foot.

Everything must be done by hand and teeth.

It has been like this for one-hundred years.

Count Marco is neither human or god.

Rumor has it Count Marco is a Reaper from the Dead Space.

A Reaper is a type of fisher who collects the disconnected spirits or "wight yaws" of the citizens of the Living End.

Count Marco would drag our wight yaws from the black waters of his black beach. Wrinkled, pallid & amphibious, our wight yaws moaned in the throes of sex and learning, flapping on the black sands of the black beach like carp not having it. Motives lost with the memory of life,

wiggle, wiggle, wiggle.

After the curse, the pace of his work slackened.

Less causes of death meant smaller swells of casualties in general.

It is said Count Marco came to the Living End to find steady employment, to right a wrong.

But we all know that by using his powers of telekinesis he is allowing death to flourish once more.

How anyone can trust a figure with giant, eczematous hands for wings and a shuriken (AKA the nightmare halo) that whirrs like a miter saw orbiting his head is beyond anyone's guess.

In the city of The Cutters—where the wheel may turn again—the knives, too, cut again.

Convenience reigns in The Cutters.
Convenience kills in The Cutters.

Needles plans to take them there.
Deep into The Cutters.

Young Steven Urn's sister Susie (Susie is a shapeshifter) and her newborn baby son have been kidnapped by Needles.

Needles is Susie's ticking time bomb of an ex-boyfriend.

He is a scrawny, naked white man with the smile of a possum. Hardened patches of sphagnum spike; dew and sweat drops glisten throughout his arms, legs, chest, and pubic area. Bruises and welts cover the naked lengths of flesh you can see past the greenie needles of sphagnum.

Needles has a limp. Needles wears it like a badge of honor. He says he earned it in a gang initiation. It comes and goes, as does the story.

He wears a gold chain around his neck. He doesn't know what the stamp '925' means.

His penis is a crusty, rolled sock.

It was Needles who told Young Steven Urn's Mother (because she has told Steven she is his mother) that he was going to take her daughter and her newborn grandchild to The Cutters where she wouldn't dare intervene or talk to him as boldly as she has.

And if you come anywhere near us, Needles warned her. *Pain will be given a home.*

Young Steven Urn's Mother does not know what to do.

If she chases after Needles she may put her daughter and grandchild at risk.

If she calls the police, her grandchild will be wrestled from the family's embrace most surely.

The journey to The Cutters is too much of a task for her aching, sagging body.

Her only choice is to ask her son, Young Steven Urn, who has recently awoken with a new anger born of chaos and innocence warped, to do *something.*

But what can he do? He is only a boy. Ten years old.

Young Steven Urn would prefer to do *nothing.*

If only Needles had taken Susie and left his newborn nephew behind, all of his problems would be solved.

Susie, his older sister, tortures him. She belittles his best efforts. Locks him in rooms.

She even tried to suffocate him with a pillow once.

Young Steven Urn cringes whenever he thinks of that pillowy suffocation and its alternate ending.

Susie never cares for her newborn child.

While Young Steven Urn and his Mother feed, clean, play, and struggle to rock the baby to sleep at night, Susie is out drinking with Needles and his spooky friends.

When Susie is home, the blinds are drawn and the lights are off. Not a peep nor a whisper.

You do not want to disturb Susie in her slumber.

Susie is a shapeshifter.

One minute she may be cheerfully lip-synching to Tom Petty.
The next she may be throwing her entire shoe collection at your
face, screaming about how she wishes the curse was lifted so she
could dig a heel into your skull.
You know, normal sister stuff.

Young Steven Urn cares for his nephew as though he were his own
child. He sees the joyfulness in the baby he often believed was a
myth. His existence is a hug.

It was Susie whom brought Needles into their lives.

Young Steven Urn interrogated Needles to great exhaustion before
the two began dating seriously.

He reminded Young Steven Urn of the fabled Skylar Deleon.

The calculations of a sociopath are lively.

Needles even insinuated or, rather, implied he had been tried for
molestation during an unexpected string of drunken confessions
between Needles and Young Steven Urn's Mother (because she has
told Steven she is his mother).
Young Steve Urn insisted their family could not risk inviting such
evil into their home. There was a baby to think about.

Sensitive airs. Fucking danger.

How this development triggered Young Steven Urn's own experienc-
es of sexual abuse can be interpreted without mention.

Susie did not listen. She was attracted to Needles' edge.
The outlaw swagger.

Now look where that attraction has gotten her.

She and her newborn baby have been kidnapped, kicking and scream-
ing, from the safety of a quiet apartment complex in a simple land
where everything must be done with your two bare hands, taken to a
city where a murder suicide is as quick as pulling the trigger thrice.

And Needles is the type to pull the trigger thrice.

—

The entrance of the city of The Cutters is otherworldly.
A pink elephant in a fez bathes itself with water flowing from its trunk.
It shakes shampoo off its pink tush and bashfully giggles like a cartoon giggles.
The pink elephant is tickled by the attention and twirls, blushing ultra.
Young Steven Urn is enchanted by the bright blinking lights.
The skyscrapers and talking billboards.
Buses—which have only existed to Young Steven Urn as artifacts from a forgotten era—screech past him.

What magic.

He has never seen them *move* before.
Helicopters and taxicabs
Bulldozers and trenchers.
Pistons spritz; the spectral rattle and hum of tiny impacts permeate the open air.
A crane pivots languidly in the distance.
A girder breaks away.

Young Steven Urn revels at the prospects of elevators.
Ascending escalators.

Count Marco's thaumaturgic energy glazes movement with a translucent layer of sparks.

A faint purple psionic sheen buzzes, spherically encasing each vehicle as they pile up against a stop light.

There is a guard at the entrance of the city of The Cutters.

The guard blocks Young Steven Urn's path and introduces himself as Ummon Shard. He is one of the thirteen Ummon Shards guarding the city's perimeter.

Ummon Shard is a colossal rhombohedral mineral.
Threads of breakage are visible.
Pieces of Ummon are concave & shattered.

There is a toll, Ummon Shard demands.

Young Steven Urn has no money and requests the fee be waived due
to the circumstances: the kidnapping of a mother and child.

Ummon quakes with laughter.

The city of The Cutters does not know compassion, he says. *Look
around you.*

Rose colored glasses wilt.

Behind Ummon, Young Steven Urn witnesses a pair of hooded and
masked men with uzis on a motorcycle with a sidecar, spray an ar-
ray of bullets at a happy-go-lucky family of three crossing the street
with lollipops.

Young Steven Urn's eyes widen with terror.

Each individual bullet sparkles with a purple psionic sheen as they
penetrate the brittle swirls of candy colors and flesh.

The men high five each other and speed off into the night, howling.

Young Steven Urn listens for the sounds of sirens.

Nothing.

Anywhere else those guns would not have been able to fire.

There is a toll, Ummon Shard demands.

What is this, a theme park for killers, Young Steven Urn asks.

You could say that, Ummon Shard quakes.

People don't just come to The Cutters to revisit the amenities of progress.
They come here to drive—and drive fast.
They come here to fly laps and drop bombs on abandoned condos.
They come here to serrate and obliterate flesh.
To do very bad things.
And Needles wants to do very bad things.

Young Steven Urn steps closer to the towering wedge of mineral. His breath fogs Ummon's face.

An army of tiny glass fleas lunge from one of Ummon's high angles.
Little nicks above the brow, in the crease of the neckline.
Young Steven Urn is covered in bites, shielding himself the best he can. Flash dancing like crazy.

You had something smart to say, Ummon drags himself toward Young Steven Urn, scraping pebbles and concrete beneath his crushing weight.

I request an audience with Count Marco!

Ummon grunts. Garbles marble.

Count Marco is the sole source of energy for the city of The Cutters. He does not have the time nor can he afford to lose focus. It would be—it would as if the world stopped turning.

The world has already stopped turning, cries Young Steven Urn. *You're living in a fantasy!*

Ummon barks from the depths of inner breakage:

PAY THE TOLL OR LEAVE HERE NOW BEFORE I GROUND YOU INTO THE GROUND.

Young Steven Urn swats at the army of glass fleas biting him, morphing them into slivers.

He is now embedded with glass fleas.

I beg of you!

I have something Count Marco desperately wants!

That's impossible. You couldn't possibly—

Young Steven Urn shakes and brushes off the last score of glass fleas, crunching the fallen with the force of his heel.

Grant me an audience with the Count and I will tell him where Ruby Bermúdez is.

—

If it's not one ridiculous dramatic freak-out it's another.

First, my wife had carried a false Chiari diagnosis for two months before meeting with a neurosurgeon who debunked the original findings.

We'd spoken with our managers at work to prepare them for unexpected absences.

We'd reached out to family and friends for support.

We'd joined online forums to gain a better understanding and obtain a semblance of a grip on what we'd perceived to be a life-changing disease.

We'd spent countless hours reading heart-wrenching testimonies of people suffering with the condition, their journeys.

We'd seen graphic post-surgery photos.

Zipper-heads they call themselves.

We did our homework.

When my wife and I had scheduled the appointment to meet with the specialist, we were gearing up to talk about surgery. We were given no reason to doubt the diagnosis.
The only option is surgery, is what the neurologist said.
And those words echoed.
The only option is surgery.
And then the neurosurgeon casually waved his wand over the results of the second MRI—the Cine MRI—and made it disappear.
Your fluid flows beautifully.
You don't have a Chiari and you don't want one, trust me.
We felt foolish. Duped even.
She still sees static and loses her balance, but at least brain surgery isn't

part of the equation anymore.

All the symptoms are still there, but at least she doesn't have to worry about identifying as a *zipper-head* anymore.

A couple of weeks later, just when we thought we were on a clear path towards resolution, my fainting spells returned.

Syncope, or *near* syncope.

I woke up one morning to go pee and, mid-stream—as though I were depleting consciousness through urination—I became severely light-headed. Flashes of hot and cold. A sickly film

coated the taste of my own mouth.

This used to happen rather frequently, so when I felt this sensation I knew to hit the ground immediately.

Last time I had these symptoms I fainted and fell between the toilet and the bathtub, convulsing.

Before that, I didn't get to the ground fast enough and collapsed like a sniper victim and pissed my boxers.

I always attributed these fits to dehydration and my bouts of heavy alcohol abuse.

But, like I said, I haven't had a drink in six months.

After two EKGs and meeting with a cardiologist, it's been established my heart rate is abnormally high.

I'd say, for a normal person, it's normal to see 40-70. But you, supine, are over 100. That isn't normal. You're in a rested position yet you might as well be running.

I'm supposed to wear a ZIO patch over my heart for 14 days to monitor for and detect any infrequent or asymptomatic arrhythmias. Afterward

I am scheduled for an echocardiogram to determine if there is anything wrong structurally.

The patch is wireless and water-resistant and can be worn comfortably under clothing.

There has been some mild itching and redness around the area, but has since subsided.

I'd say my only concern is now I'm too aware of my own heart.

I can feel the monitor there above it and, beneath the monitor, I know my heart is there and it is beating fast. Maybe faster now that I'm anxious in my constant recognition of its inhabitance.

Maybe even faster now as I'm growing paranoid that my thinking about it is making it beat faster and the faster it beats the closer I get to that gauntlet punch in the chest they call a heart attack.

I think my grandfather died of a heart attack.

This feels like a twisted game of hot potato [widow edition] between my wife and I.

The small bushes of gray in my brown beard have since grown white.

Is it the sprouting imposition of age, or am I a ghost, Dear Reader; a high potency of terror screaming from the Netherlands of a microverse.

Parts of me can be a ghost, can't they?

Imposter limbs and statement of self.

We have gone there.

"Ummon Shard has informed me of your intelligence to the where-abouts of Ruby Bermúdez," Count Marco says, levitating above his throne built of twisted and compacted cubes of skeletons and aluminum cannery.

His giant eczematous hand-wings fidget and twiddle, tearing at hangnails. The fingers—engorged, fleshy lumber—flick torn pieces of skin, falling like feathers.

Count Marco's arms are crossed. He is analyzing—taking in his new visitor.

When he speaks, his speech is voiceless, yet the words are still somehow there, creeping like the nightmare halo whirring sinisterly behind Young Steven Urn.

With the slightest thought, Count Marco can multiply the size of the shuriken and saw Young Steven Urn in half.

"Such intelligence interests me. So, for now, Young Steven Urn, you interest me."

Although Ruby Bermúdez's role as Overseer of the Living End precedes the current order (there is none), they refuse to relinquish the earpiece commlink assigned to them. It is a tool issued by the Fryspunkt Council to be given to all Overseers as a means to communicate and govern their assigned prospective rims within the Dammit Hole.

Ruby Bermúdez was terminated as Overseer after X. Ikaroa granted the immortal Michael Quartz his most ridiculous wish.

X. Ikaroa should have never had the access to manipulate the laws of the Living End at such a grand, planetary scale. A detrimental oversight of the Bermúdez administration.

Ruby Bermúdez is also directly responsible for the Cerise Gallery Massacre.

One evening, while Ruby Bermudez was hiding from the Fryspunkt Council in another rim of the Dammit Hole far from our own, they were too busy indulging in a round of Sailor Moon cosplay and, because they could not be bothered by the constant prayers for recognition and praise by the now infamous poet and curator, Noah Fang Quicksilver, they hurriedly and carelessly sent him the egg of a demonic and prodigious Hercules beetle to temper the distraction.

Noah Fang Quicksilver murdered and sacrificed his rivals and friends to the egg, its instar, pupae, and beetle until he absorbed all of their talents and skills.

We have grown a century since then but nothing has changed.

The only way the Living End can heal is with a change in administration.

Count Marco needs Ruby's earpiece to restore order to the Living End and the Dead Space. His vision or plans may be unclear, but what is crystal--he will stop at nothing.

"May I ask how you came upon this intelligence?"

"They told me," says Young Steven Urn.

"What do you mean they told you?" Count Marco asks, he uncrosses his arms and lowers himself onto the throne.

"They speak to me and I can hear them. I hear many things." Young Steven Urn deviates his observant eye from Count Marco and drafts a faculty of presence in these chambers he loosely defines to himself as a shaken condominium.

"What is it you hear?"

"I am not a prophet. I have no knowledge. I only hear things, things spoken to me and to me alone, from the past, the present, and the future..."

"And it is Ruby Bermúdez who speaks to you?"

"Yes."

"What does Ruby speak?"

"Ruby... Ruby speaks to me in prayer."

"In prayer?"

"Yes. It is Ruby who is praying to me. Well, not me. Ruby prays to the god I will become, and I can hear that conversation."

"Can you participate in this conversation?"

"Not now, as it is not I who Ruby is speaking to. Ruby is speaking to the god I will become."

"Though it is from this conversation or prayer you've overheard you have gained the location of Ruby Bermúdez?"

"The location they will be at."

"When?"

"Twenty years."

"This is preposterous, Young Steven Urn! I should split you in two!"

"How you respond in this moment will affect how I choose to respond to Ruby when Ruby asks for my help."

"Your help!? From what!? Besides, you are only a mortal!"

"I am a mortal now. But there will be a time when I am not a mortal, in death maybe, and your reign will spread and you, Count Marco, will come face-to-face with Ruby Bermúdez, who will be seeking my aid. How you respond today dictates the course of your achievements twenty years from now."

"This is a unique form of intelligence, Young Steven Urn. What is your proposition?"

"For you, Count Marco, to permit my entrance to The Cutters free of charge. For you to temporarily turn off your powers of thaumaturgy, let the city of The Cutters sleep and bestow upon me a handicap; the advantage of weidling any weapon of my choice to takedown Needles, the man who is holding my sister Susie and her son, my nephew, captive in the bowels of The Cutters."

"And by letting the city sleep, you will come to my aid when you are a god, not Ruby's, twenty years from now, which will guarantee me the commlink and thus, the entirety of the Living End and Dead Space?"

"Yes, I will owe you one."

Count Marco claps his two pairs of hands together, a column of wind nearly knocks Young Steven Urn off his feet.

"You have yourself a deal. Regardless of the outcome, I am looking forward to how you handle yourself. You may be able to drive a car when Needles can't, and you may be able to shoot a gun when Needles can't, but if he gets his touch on you, that's all you."

"I'm not worried," Young Steven Urn stares back at Count Marco with a gaze that exudes a complete willingness and utmost eagerness to lose oneself to the madness of animalistic rage.

"Teleconnect me back to the streets."

—

Rage launches Young Steven Urn into the grungy, obliteratingly pro-dromal streets of the city of The Cutters; soggy with newspapers and clumps of mysterious lint, en masse; spongy, tobacco stained foam mattresses; entire wardrobes discarded, flattened into the asphalt as if they were ironed there.

Obscene squishy sounds echo throughout the hidden connections of back alleyways.

Young Steven Urn is a beastly flash, prowling voraciously with the heavy panting of volcanic rock, eyes aglow with a polarizing storm; an avalanche of sky, oblivion cries.

He is invincible.

The steel toe boots implant a bombastic, threatening punctuation in his step. They do not slow him down.

He swings his metal bat, smashing windows and receptacles in his path.

A hunchback and crooked, spindly figure wrapped in an orange sleeping bag spooks up on him with a switchblade and thrusts at his stomach.

There is only a small indent. No visible scratch or drop of blood.

Young Steven Urn bats at the man's jaw. Teeth and broken bone spill out onto the street like tackle. Their head spins. Their neck snaps.

Rage carries Young Steven Urn over the sprawled out tangle of a beaten corpse.

Rage carries Young Steven Urn down wide turns, up cobblestone hills, and into the parking garage below Needles' apartment unit, where he holds bunker.

Rage carries Young Steven Urn past the lines of leaning tents posted in abandoned parking spots. The rage guides him to the elevator where the doors magically part for him. Young Steven Urn pushes the button for the fourth floor.

Rage carries Young Steven Urn through the parted elevator doors.

The rage carries him down a hallway painted red.

The rage carries Young Steven Urn through a smashed and splintered door.

Suddenly, as if the entire time he was viewing a demo of a first-person shooter, detached from play, and Young Steven Urn mistakenly hit a button, joining the game; unfamiliar with the inverted control style, displaced by the change of environment and fearful of the predicament of knowing what his character can do, yet completely ignorant of how to do any of it, Young Steven Urn stands dead center in the throes of Needles' living quarters.

"Before we begin," Young Steven Urn says, slowly approaching Needles, who is snorting a line of green powder off the coffee table. "Did you touch him?"

Needles laughs, puffs of green powder form a cloud around him.

Needles rises through the cloud, still laughing, chuckling.

He is naked. The sphagnum on his greasy, emaciated body glistens like olivenite.

"Slow down, tough guy," Needles says. He tries to suck up the cloud of green as if it were smoke and he could blow rings with it.

"I only told your mother that shit to get under her skin. Looks like it worked, too. I'm living in her skin. I'm a mother-fucking snake."

Needles hisses.

"Where is my sister? Where is my nephew?"

"In the other room, hanging out."

Needles points to a room beyond the kitchen.

Young Steven Urn lifts the metal bat and presses it against Needles' chest.

"Stay," he demands.

He walks to the room beyond the kitchen. There he finds his sister Susie and his nephew sitting cross-legged on the floor, playing peek-a-boo in dim light.

Susie pauses.

"Look at you, tough guy! What are you doing here?"

"I'm here for my nephew. I'm taking him back home."

Susie scooches awkwardly across the hardwood floor in an attempt to uncross her legs. She stands and scoops Young Steven Urn's prize nephew off the floor.

"What a coincidence! We were leaving anyway. Mom refuses to send us any money and Needles is so boring!"

Young Steven Urn stares blankly in astonishment.

"You weren't kidnapped?"

Susie hacks a singular laugh,

"Are you kidding me? No, we weren't kidnapped, we just wanted money!"

Young Steven Urn places the metal bat onto the bed beside him and rests his tired frame against the red wall of the room beyond the kitchen.

"But mom's broke, Susie. We live in low income housing and we're on food stamps! All this drama was for essentially nothing!?"

Susie scowls and holds her baby toward him.

"Yep, I guess all this drama *was* for nothing!"

Ten years later the man who Needles is based on showed up in a suit and tie with two kids dangling on his sleeves, an extra chin, grainy stubble, and had changed his name to something Gaelic.

I was working at the pawnshop then and for a moment the only item I was concerned with defining was a plain, white gold wedding band.

I scratched it against the small black stone, dropped the acid on the mark and set it on the scale for its weight in grams.

It wasn't until I compared the photo on the ID to the man standing on the other side of the register that the realization stung me; like tiny little needles, it stung me.

I said nothing. I did my very best to conceal my animosity.

But it was him.

The man who, with the help of my sister, tore the one dignified and pure aspect of my family apart.

Shortly after the events *loosely* dramatized in the previous story, my nephew became a vivid blip on CPS's radar and, with the ease of a key stroke, had been transitioned to live with his grandparents on his father's side on Whidbey Island.

I was ten years old, overtly familiarizing myself with the contours of a premature mental breakdown. I became resentful and defiant. I became a violent pyromaniac. I dropped out of sixth grade and fled to arcades. I fed my life to as much make-believe as possible. I went as far as making up an evil, mischievous twin (as a means to cope with the real-life twin I had been told my mother miscarried, whose existence was then denied to me when I reached adulthood) and moved in with my estranged father in Monterey, CA, where all I did was cry the tears of everything that was going on and call my step-mother a bitch until they had enough of me and sent me back in boxes.

There he was, the very finger that pushed the dominoes, dazed within the confines of an impatient mind while I calculated the appropriate amount to loan him.

How could he not remember me?

Say nothing?

All the times I'd swing the bat at him. Bust a whole in something easy, to make it look easy.

I fantasized about memorizing his address as I confirmed it with him.

I thought of tying him up and recording footage of him confessing to the abuse he inflicted on my sister, for tormenting my mother, my nephew, and myself for entertainment purposes.

I would play the footage for his family so that no matter how kind he'd been to them, the new leaf, turned, they would see the imposter; the needle, shimmering brightly in the amber haystack of his deceit.

The remaining details of the transaction and minor dialogue shared between us are irrelevant.

In the end, he left. I excused myself from the loan counter and splashed cold water on my face in the bathroom. I chain smoked cigarettes for lunch.

If we forward to today, July 18th, 2017, I can tell you that the separation from my nephew is among the many incidents in which I have yet found closure. However, I have come close.

My nephew, who is no longer a baby, has made contact with his mother and is slowly integrating himself back into our toxic clan.

I am by no means rushing the process, but there has been at least one failed attempt to reunite.

Waiting is hard.

I am aware the expectation that upon seeing him I will somehow be clean again is unrealistic. I'm only acknowledging that a piece that was once lost may soon be returned to me.

I don't even know where to begin. I'm concerned with the images that may resurface when he sees my face.

Have the actions of my former, younger self, brilliant with rage, contributed to a pain he may now be grappling with as a new adult?

Or will he remember the stuffed animals and gentle noogies?

The quiet coos.

Over time I've learned to think in rattlesnakes and appreciate the cupcakes as they come (which due to certain conditioning, I'm constantly convinced are poisoned).

To Be Continued…

C. C. Hannett is the author of *Triune + I Gave This Dream to a Color* (Spuyten Duyvil). In a past-life he curated hybrid/cross-genre literary events and published chapbooks with both Shotgun Wedding and Horse Less Press. Current work has been placed with *Softblow*, *Gimmick*, *Punch Drunk*, and *Nada*. Stay tuned for his collection, *SAGA ctrl*.

You can reach him at

topazglue AT gmail DOT com

Made in the USA
Monee, IL
07 July 2026